Artisan Patisserie for the Home Baker

Avner Laskin

Artisan Patisserie for the Home Baker

Avner Laskin

Sterling Publishing Co., Inc.
New York

Edited by Shoshana Brickman
Culinary editing by Phyllis Glazer
Design and layout by TAG Concept Ltd.

Photograph on page 4   © Pierre Herme, Paris
Photograph on pages ii, 31, 169   © Elan Penn

Library of Congress Cataloging-in-Publication Data
Laskin, Avner.
Artisan patisserie for the home baker / Avner Laskin.
p. cm.
ISBN-13: 978-1-4027-2408-4
ISBN-10: 1-4027-2408-X
1. PastryóEurope. 2. DessertsóEurope. I. Title.

TX773.L3184 2006
641.8'65094—dc22

2006047510

2   4   6   8   10   9   7   5   3   1

Published by Sterling Publishing Co., Inc.
387 Park Avenue South, New York, NY 10016
© 2006 by Penn Publishing Ltd.
Distributed in Canada by Sterling Publishing
c/o Canadian Manda Group, 165 Dufferin Street,
Toronto, Ontario, Canada M6K 3H6
Distributed in the United Kingdom by GMC Distribution Services,
Castle Place, 166 High Street, Lewes, East Sussex, England BN7 1XU
Distributed in Australia by Capricorn Link (Australia) Pty. Ltd.
P.O. Box 704, Windsor, NSW 2756, Australia

Printed in China
All rights reserved

Sterling ISBN-13: 978-1-4027-2408-4
ISBN-10: 1-4027-2408-X

For information about custom editions, special sales, premium and
corporate purchases, please contact Sterling Special Sales
Department at 800-805-5489 or specialsales@sterlingpub.com.

To my family, Rachel and Danya,

who inspired and supported me

throughout this project

Table of Contents

Introduction

For me, baking is a sensual and magical process, and the marvelous scent of freshly baked goods is my strongest sense-memory of home. Patisserie is an art: it involves the finest ingredients and painstaking precision, all coaxed together into creations to please all the senses.

During the years that I studied in France and traveled through Europe, I discovered that the world of patisserie is not exclusively French. Each country has evolved its own expression of the art, with flavors and textures that make it different from the rest.

In this book, you'll find my collection of favorite recipes from France, Portugal, Spain, and Italy, where patisserie is a way of life. In recent years, quality patisserie is becoming a trend in America as well, with an increasing number of creative chefs across the country blending novel and native ingredients with traditional techniques.

But in truth — there's nothing like the freshness, taste, and personal satisfaction you'll experience when you make these luscious classic creations in your own kitchen. I guarantee your family will rave, and your friends will find excuses to visit more often. It is possible.

Although I bake professionally, all the recipes in this book were prepared in my home kitchen, and any recipe that didn't seem practical to produce at home was rejected. Some of the recipes are easy; others are more challenging. I have placed the most challenging recipes in the last two chapters of the book. By the time you reach those pages, you will have lots of experience in the art of patisserie. Once you understand the basic techniques and principles involved in creating the classics, you can express your own imagination and creativity as you bake.

It's important to remember, however, that baking is an exact science, and that the process is sometimes complicated. You can make life a lot easier, and your finished product better, if you read carefully through the recipe, and prepare measured ingredients, equipment, and utensils on the work surface, before you begin. You'll often find that some parts of the recipe can be prepared in advance, like crème patisserie, marzipan, or one of the other recipes in the Basics chapter. Organize your prep time accordingly, and set a pace that suits your lifestyle.

Take the time to enjoy both the preparation and the consumption. My family and I have enjoyed every moment — and every bite. We hope you do too!

Avner Laskin

Essentials & Basic Recipes

I always remind my students to read through a recipe from beginning to end, and make sure they have all the ingredients and utensils on hand, before they begin. Although this is important in all forms of baking, it is particularly true when creating patisserie.

In addition to standard baking pans and sheets, you'll also be using items like baking rings, cellophane cake collars, parchment paper, pastry bags, and tips. Using these specialty items will make a world of difference in the final product.

Today more than ever, you can find these items at reasonable prices, in specialty stores and catalogues, or by ordering online.

Important Tips

> Always preheat the oven for 30 minutes before baking. I recommend preheating to about 10% higher than the recipe calls for, and reducing the heat to the required temperature when placing the product in the oven.

> Use the convection setting option in your oven for all recipes, especially if baking several items together. If you do not own a convection oven, you can bake in a regular oven, but allow 20%–30% more baking time.

> Place the baking pan/s on the middle rack in the center of the oven for even baking.

> Note that using a different pan than called for in the recipe will affect baking time. For example, if the recipe calls for small pans and you use a large pan, baking time will be extended.

> For best results, make certain that all the ingredients you use are the freshest and finest available.

   > Fruit should be ripe, but not overripe.
   > Milk and eggs should be very fresh—check last date of sale.
   > All eggs should be large. Use cold eggs, straight from the refrigerator, unless otherwise stated.
   > Use only fine natural vanilla extract.
   > Use quality chocolate with at least 50% cocoa solids.
   > Use only high quality cocoa.
   > Use only fresh creamery butter, no substitutions.

> To defrost frozen dough, place on a work surface and let thaw at room temperature. If the frozen dough has already been rolled out in a quiche or tart pan, do not defrost before using. Pre-bake by placing a round of parchment paper in the center, top it with a commercial weight or beans, and bake according to the recipe directions.

> To defrost frozen mousse cakes, let stand at room temperature for 30 minutes before serving.

> Always use a clean and dry bowl to beat egg whites.

> For best results, melt chocolate in a double boiler. Keep the water in the bottom pot at a steady simmer, and do not allow it to touch the underside of the top pot. Stir only at the end. If you don't have a double boiler, you can substitute by placing the chocolate pieces in a bowl over a pan of simmering water.

> When cooking water and sugar to make syrup, do not stir the mixture while it is cooking.

> When adding whipped substances such as whole eggs, egg whites, or egg yolks to dry substances such as flour, ground almonds, or cocoa, use a wide rubber spatula and fold in with wide movements.

> Always store cookies in an airtight jar at room temperature, unless otherwise stated.

Baking Pans & Utensils

I recommend using nonstick or silicone baking pans, because they are easy to clean and save on greasing. The pans we'll be using include the following:

> **10-inch fluted tart/quiche pan** with removable bottom, for tarts and family-sized quiches.

> **4-inch fluted tartlet/quiche pans** with removable bottoms, for individual servings.

  Note: Recipes calling for a 10-inch tart pan with removable bottom may be baked in six 4-inch individual tartlet pans.

> **8-inch kugelhopf pan** for batter cakes and family-sized yeast pastries.

> **4-inch kugelhopf pan** for individual servings.

  Note: Recipes calling for an 8-inch Kugelhopf pan may be baked in five 4-inch Kugelhopf pans.

> **2 1/2-inch French brioche mold** for individual batter and yeast cakes.

> **12-cup muffin pan**

> **Regular or disposable 12-inch aluminum loaf pans**

> **3-inch baking cups** preferably made of brown parchment paper or aluminum.

> **10-inch and 8-inch springform pans**

> **10 x 2 1/2-inch baking rings** for family-sized cakes. Springform pans with removal bottoms may be substituted.

> **3 x 2 1/2-inch baking rings** for individual cakes.

> **Madeleine pan** for making scallop-shaped mini-cakes, used for traditional madeleine cakes or any batter cake recipe.

> **Baking sheet** that can fit into your refrigerator.

> **Wire rack** for cooling.

> **Silicone baking sheet**

Essential Accessories

> **Parchment paper** for lining pans and baking sheets, and as insulation for cakes containing layers of cream or mousse. Sheets of parchment paper are preferable to a roll.

> **Clear 2-inch ✗ 28 1/2-inch cellophane cake collars** for lining the inside of baking rings. These are essential for protecting the edges of mousse and cream cakes, and for facilitating their removal from baking rings.

> **Pastry brush** preferably with long soft bristles.

> **Rolling pin** for rolling out pastry dough. If you are buying a new rolling pin, I recommend 18-inch aluminum or nonstick rolling pins.

> **Strong, good quality egg whisk** for beating and emulsifying ingredients when an electric mixer isn't necessary.

> **Wide rubber or silicone spatula with wooden handle** for really getting to the bottom of the bowl. Also important for folding in ingredients.

> **Candy thermometer** that measures more than 400°F. This will also help keep your caramel from burning.

> **Measuring cups and spoons** for accurate measurement.

> **Long-handled wooden spoon** that can be used to mixing, and for forming Almond Tuiles (page 88).

> **Ceramic pie weights** to help keep flaky pie crusts or quiche shells from bubbling up when pre-baking or "baking blind." You'll need 2 pounds of weights. Ceramic weights are preferable to metal weights, and more hygienic for keeping. In a pinch, use a round of parchment paper weighed down with rice or beans. Discard after use.

> **Serrated knife** for cutting baked products without ruining their texture.

> **10-inch chef's knife** with a broad, tapered shape and fine edge. Also called a French knife.

> **4-inch wide stainless steel spatula** is especially handy for making chocolate curls, scraping kneading boards, and picking up ingredients from flat surfaces.

> **12-inch palette knife with rounded top** is useful for working with moist substances like pastry cream and mousse.

> **20-inch pastry bag** for piping icing. I like this length because it has enough space and never leaks. I recommend using silicone pastry bags, if available, since these are easy to clean and don't absorb colors, odors, or flavors.

> **Stainless steel pastry tip set** with various sizes and shapes of tips. These sets can be found in outlets, large department stores, specialty kitchen stores, through catalogues, and online.

Basic Recipes

In the following pages, you'll find recipes for pastry crusts, fillings, sauces, and more that we'll be using in recipes throughout the book. Note that the recipes in this chapter do not include baking instructions—you'll find these in the final recipes in which they appear.

If you're making Quiche Lorraine (page 130), for example, you'll find that the recipe calls for both the Savory Shortcrust Pastry and the Basic Quiche Filling described in this chapter. Since there are many items that may be prepared in advance and kept frozen or refrigerated until needed, it's a good idea to read through all the necessary recipes before you begin, and coordinate when and how you'll make them. This can make your life considerably easier, and help shorten preparation time.

I know that several of the items in this chapter may be bought ready-made, but there is nothing quite like the taste, quality, freshness, and sensual pleasure of making them by yourself from scratch.

Basic Shortcrust Pastry

This classic version of shortcrust pastry is used for pies, cookies and desserts like Tarte Tatin (page 34).

Makes enough for one 10-inch tart

1/2 cup cold butter

2 tablespoons sugar

1 egg

1 tablespoon cold water

1/2 teaspoon salt

1 1/4 cups unbleached all-purpose flour

(1) Combine the butter and sugar in the bowl of a food processor and process 2 minutes until smooth, stopping occasionally and wiping down the sides with a rubber spatula, if necessary.

(2) Stop the processor, add the egg, water, and salt and process an additional 2 minutes, until smooth and uniform in texture.

(3) Stop the processor again, add the flour, and continue to process 1 minute until a neat ball is formed. Remove the dough from the work bowl and cover with plastic wrap. Let rest in the refrigerator for at least 1 hour before using.

Note: Dough may be frozen for up to 2 months. Defrost at room temperature before using.

Almond Shortcrust Pastry

This best-ever version of shortcrust pastry is used to complement tarts with rich flavors like chocolate, passion fruit, and pineapple. It can also be used for making Paris-Brest (page 64) and Peruvian Chocolate Alfajores (page 94).

Makes enough for one 10-inch tart

1/2 cup cold butter

1/4 cup confectioner's sugar

1/4 cup ground blanched almonds

1 egg

1 tablespoon cold water

1/2 teaspoon salt

1 cup unbleached all-purpose flour

(1) Combine the butter with half of the confectioner's sugar in the bowl of a food processor and process 2 minutes to form a smooth mass.

(2) Stop the processor, add the almonds and the remaining confectioner's sugar, and process 2 minutes until smooth.

(3) Stop the processor again and add the egg, water, salt, and half the flour. Continue to process 2 minutes, until the dough is smooth and uniform. Add the remaining flour and process 1 minute until a neat ball is formed.

(4) Remove the dough from the bowl and cover with plastic wrap. Let rest in the refrigerator for at least 1 hour before using.

Note: Dough may be frozen for up to 2 months. Defrost at room temperature before using.

Variation: For Chocolate-Almond Shortcrust Pastry, add 1 tablespoon of cocoa to Step 2.

Savory Shortcrust Pastry

This shortcrust pastry is used for savory pastries like cheese or vegetable quiche.

Makes enough for one 10-inch tart

1/2 cup cold butter

1/2 teaspoon salt

1 egg

1 tablespoon cold water

1 1/4 cups unbleached all-purpose flour

(1) Place the butter and salt in the bowl of a food processor and process 2 minutes until thoroughly combined.

(2) Stop the processor and add the egg, water, and half the flour. Continue to process 2 minutes, until the dough is smooth and uniform.

(3) Stop the processor again, add the remaining flour, and continue to process 1 minute until a neat ball is formed.

(4) Remove the dough from the bowl and cover with plastic wrap. Let rest in the refrigerator for at least 1/2 hour before using.

Note: Dough may be frozen for up to 2 months. Defrost at room temperature before using.

Puff Pastry

Made with butter rather than margarine, this fine puff pastry is easy to make and rich in flavor. You'll be using it for Mille-Feuilles (pages 134 and 136), and many other recipes in this book.

Makes enough for three 10-inch tarts

1 cup water

1/2 tablespoon salt

1/3 cup melted butter

3 1/4 cups unbleached all-purpose flour

1 1/4 cups cold butter

(1) Combine the water, salt, melted butter, and flour in the bowl of a standing mixer. Mix on low speed using a dough hook for 5 minutes, or until the dough is smooth and uniform.

(2) Remove the dough from the mixer and form it into a ball. Wrap in plastic wrap and chill in the refrigerator for 1 hour.

(3) Working on a floured surface, use a rolling pin to roll out the dough into a 10-inch circle.

(4) Wrap the cold butter in parchment paper, pound it down lightly with a rolling pin, then roll it into a 6 inch square. Remove the parchment paper and place the butter in the center of the dough. Fold in the edges of the dough to cover the butter completely.

(5) Lightly sprinkle flour over the dough and roll it out again to form a 20 x 10-inch rectangle. Fold the long sides inward, to form a 10-inch square, then fold in half to form a 10 x 5-inch rectangle. Wrap in plastic wrap and place in the refrigerator to rest for 30 minutes.

(6) Remove from the refrigerator and repeat Step 5. Chill for 30 minutes before using.

Note: If making larger quantities of puff pastry, always work with the same ratio of butter to flour.

Choux Paste

This is a classic of European baking, used for making cream puffs, éclairs, and traditional cakes like Paris-Brest (page 64), and Saint-Honoré (page 66).

Makes enough for about 25 éclairs

1/2 cup water

1/2 cup milk (not nonfat)

1/2 cup butter

1 tablespoon sugar

1/2 teaspoon salt

1 cup unbleached all-purpose flour

4 eggs

(1) Combine the water, milk, butter, sugar, and salt in a small saucepan and bring to a boil over medium heat.

(2) Stir in the flour and cook over low heat, stirring constantly, until the mixture forms a ball.

(3) Transfer the hot dough to the bowl of an electric mixer and beat on low speed for 3 minutes to cool slightly.

(4) Add the eggs one at a time, beating well after each addition to blend in each egg before adding the next.

(5) Cover the bowl with plastic wrap and chill for at least 30 minutes in the refrigerator before using. Store covered in the refrigerator for up to 24 hours.

Note: This dough is generally piped onto the baking tray using a pastry bag.

Basic Génoise Torte

This light sponge cake is a base for many cakes, including Black Forest Cake and Sacher Torte. In this book, we'll be using it to make luscious strawberry cake—the Fraisier (page 152).

Makes enough for one 10-inch baking ring

4 eggs

1 egg yolk

1/2 cup sugar

2/3 cup unbleached all-purpose flour

(1) Combine the eggs, egg yolk, and sugar in the top of a double boiler. Using a wire balloon whisk or an electric hand mixer, whisk the mixture until it reaches 110°F.

(2) Remove from heat and beat until thick and firm.

(3) Gradually fold in the flour with a rubber spatula.

(4) The génoise is now ready for use. Use immediately, according to individual recipe instructions.

Note: For best results, use a candy thermometer to check the temperature of the egg-sugar mixture.

Ladyfinger Mixture

Most people think ladyfingers are light, finger-shaped cakes. Although this is true, the same mixture is also used in professional patisserie to layer or wrap mousse cakes. This recipe makes two cakes rather than one, as I find halving the recipe has a negative effect on the texture. I suggest making recipes that use this mixture when you're expecting a large crowd.

Makes enough for two large mousse cakes

4 eggs, separated

1/2 cup sugar

2/3 cup unbleached all-purpose flour

(1) Whip the egg whites until creamy in the bowl of an electric mixer.

(2) Gradually add 1/4 cup of the sugar and continue beating until stiff.

(3) In a separate bowl, whip the egg yolks and the remaining 1/4 cup of sugar till creamy. Gently fold the egg yolk mixture and flour into the egg whites using a rubber spatula. Mix until smooth.

(4) Use immediately, according to individual recipe instructions.

Variation: To add a touch of chocolate flavor, add 1 tablespoon of cocoa to the flour.

Dacquoise Mixture

This rich almond-flavored sponge cake is also used to layer or wrap mousse cakes. As in the Ladyfinger Mixture, this recipe makes two cakes rather than one, because whipping only 2 egg whites negatively affects the texture.

Makes enough for two large mousse cakes

4 eggs whites

1/4 cup sugar

1/3 cup ground blanched almonds

2 tablespoons unbleached all-purpose flour

(1) Whip the egg whites till creamy in the bowl of an electric mixer.

(2) Gradually add the sugar and continue beating until stiff.

(3) Gradually fold in the almonds and flour using a rubber spatula. Mix gently until smooth.

(4) Use immediately, according to individual recipe instructions.

Italian Meringue Mixture

Italian-style meringue is one of the most basic and important recipes for the professional patissière. It is excellent for separating the layers in mousse cakes, for making meringue cookies, and for topping Lemon Tarts (page 44).

Makes enough for one mousse cake

2 tablespoons water

1 cup sugar

4 egg whites

(1) Place the water in a small saucepan and add the sugar.

(2) Cook over medium heat until the mixture reaches 250°F. Do not stir.

(3) In the meantime, whip the egg whites with an electric mixer until soft peaks form.

(4) With the mixer running, gradually add the sugar mixture, and continue whipping for 10 to 15 minutes, until the mixture reaches room temperature.

(5) Use immediately, according to individual recipe directions.

Note: For best results, use a candy thermometer to check the temperature of the water-sugar mixture.

Royal Chocolate Frosting

The addition of glucose gives this frosting an ultra-smooth texture, makes it easy to work with, and helps it stay fresh far longer than regular chocolate frosting. Guaranteed to please every chocolate lover!

Makes about 4 cups, enough to frost two 10-inch cakes

1/2 cup water

1/2 cup sugar

9 ounces bittersweet chocolate, cut in small pieces

2 tablespoons vegetable oil

1/4 cup glucose

3/4 cup heavy cream

(1) Mix the water and sugar in a small saucepan, and bring to a boil. Do not stir. Remove from heat and set aside.

(2) Melt the chocolate in the top of a double boiler over low heat. Make sure the water does not touch the bottom of the bowl.

(3) When the chocolate is fully melted, add the oil and glucose. Mix well.

(4) Stir in the heavy cream and mix well.

(5) Blend the water-sugar mixture into the melted chocolate and remove from heat. Cool, cover, and store in the refrigerator for up to 1 week. To soften, gently heat in the top of a double boiler.

Chocolate Ganache

Ganache (pronounced gah-NAHSH), is a delicious combination of chocolate and cream that can be used as a layer in mousse cake, as the basis for chocolate mousse or hot chocolate, or as a smooth glossy coating on cake. When chilled, it can be formed into chocolate truffles.

Makes 2 cups

1 cup heavy cream

7 ounces bittersweet chocolate, cut in small pieces

(1) Pour the heavy cream into a small saucepan and bring just to the boiling point.

(2) Place the chocolate in a bowl and pour over the cream. Mix well, cover, and let cool to room temperature. Before using, chill in a covered container in the refrigerator until firm. May be stored in an airtight container in the refrigerator for up to 1 week.

Crème Patissière

Crème Patissière—pastry cream—is one of the important basics that every pastry chef needs to know. We use it alone, or in combination with other ingredients, to fill éclairs, cream puffs, tarts, petits fours, and many other French pastries.

Makes about 3 cups

2 cups milk

1/2 cup sugar

6 egg yolks

2 tablespoons cornstarch

(1) Combine the milk and 1/4 cup of the sugar in a small saucepan and bring to a boil.

(2) In the meantime, whisk the egg yolks, the remaining 1/4 cup sugar, and cornstarch in a small bowl till smooth.

(3) Once the milk has boiled, reduce to the lowest possible heat and slowly add the egg yolk mixture, whisking constantly with a wire whisk until the mixture bubbles and thickens to the consistency of cooked farina. Remove from heat.

(4) Transfer the pastry cream to a clean dry container, and cover with plastic wrap to prevent contact with air. Let cool to room temperature, then place in the refrigerator till fully chilled. Use within 2 days.

Crème Anglaise

This custard sauce is often flavored with vanilla or liqueur. It makes a delicious accompaniment to the Tarte Tatin (page 34), and can be used as a basis for baked puddings.

Makes about 3 cups

2 cups milk

1/2 cup sugar

1 vanilla pod, split lengthwise

6 egg yolks

2 teaspoons pure vanilla extract, 5 ounces melted bittersweet chocolate, or 1 tablespoon liqueur, optional

(1) In a small saucepan, bring the milk, 1/4 cup of the sugar, and the vanilla pod just to a boil over medium heat.

(2) In the meantime, whisk the egg yolks and the remaining 1/4 cup of sugar in a separate bowl till smooth.

(3) Once the milk boils, reduce to lowest possible heat. Quickly whisk 1/3 of the boiling milk mixture into the egg mixture and beat constantly to blend. Pour the egg-milk mixture back into the saucepan, whisking constantly.

(4) Continue cooking over low heat, stirring with a wooden spoon, until the mixture reaches 175°F.

(5) Remove from heat and strain through a fine mesh strainer into a clean bowl. While the mixture is still warm, add the vanilla extract, chocolate, or liqueur.

(6) Place the bowl over an ice-filled bowl and stir for 10 minutes, or until the crème cools to room temperature. Cover and refrigerate for at least 2 hours, or up to 2 days.

Note: For best results, use a candy thermometer to check the temperature of the egg-milk mixture.

Basic Quiche Filling

By adding your favorite ingredients to this basic filling, you can develop a trademark quiche of your own.

Makes enough to fill one 10-inch quiche or six 4-inch individual quiches

3 eggs

1 1/4 cups heavy cream

1 teaspoon salt

1/2 teaspoon freshly grated nutmeg

(1) Combine the eggs and heavy cream in a bowl and mix gently.

(2) Whisk in the salt and nutmeg till smooth.

(3) Use immediately or transfer to a covered container and refrigerate for up to 2 days.

Almond Crème

This cream is multipurpose. It can be used to fill Danish pastries, cakes like Pithiviers (page 138), or as a foundation layer in sweet tarts.

Makes enough to fill one 10-inch tart

1/2 cup butter

1/2 cup sugar

2 eggs

2/3 cup ground blanched almonds

1/2 teaspoon pure vanilla extract

1/2 teaspoon Amaretto

(1) Place the butter in the top of a double boiler. Melt over medium heat.

(2) Remove from heat and whisk in the sugar and eggs. Blend till smooth.

(3) Mix in the almonds, vanilla, and Amaretto.

(4) Cover and refrigerate for at least 30 minutes, or up to 2 days.

Apricot Glaze

A snap to make, this glaze—called *nappage* in French—enhances the natural color of baked goods, making them look fresh from the oven even hours after baking.

Makes about 5 cups

1 cup water

2 cups sugar

1 (15-ounce) can apricots in heavy syrup

3 Golden Delicious apples, coarsely chopped (with peel and seeds)

1 tablespoon powdered pectin

(1) Combine the water, sugar, apricots and syrup, and chopped apples in a large saucepan and bring to a boil over high heat.

(2) Lower heat and stir in the pectin. Cook on low heat for 1 1/2 hours.

(3) Strain the mixture through a fine mesh strainer, and let cool to room temperature.

(4) Cover and store in the refrigerator for up to 6 months.

Red Currant Glaze

This glaze is perfect for enhancing the look and flavor of cakes topped with red or purple fruit. Even if hours have passed since baking, it will give any berry-filled cake a bright, fresh-baked look.

Makes about 4 cups

1 cup water

1 cup sugar

1 pound frozen mixed berries

1 tablespoon powdered pectin

(1) Combine the water, sugar, and berries in a large saucepan and bring to a boil over high heat, stirring occasionally.

(2) Lower heat and stir in the pectin. Cook on low heat for 1 1/2 hours.

(3) Strain the mixture through a fine mesh strainer and let cool to room temperature.

(4) Cover and store in the refrigerator for up to 6 months.

Coffee Essence

Just a little bit of this concentrated syrup adds the tempting aroma of good coffee to any mousse, crème, or even dough. You can also fortify the syrup with some good quality coffee liqueur.

Makes about 3 cups

1 cup sugar

1 cup plus 1 tablespoon water

1/2 cup premium instant coffee

(1) Mix the sugar with 1 tablespoon water and cook on medium-low heat, until the sugar turns a dark caramel color. Do not stir.

(2) Lower heat and stir in the remaining 1 cup of water. Cook, stirring often, until well blended.

(3) Add the instant coffee, mix well, and cook over low heat for 5 minutes.

(4) Cool slightly and pour into a clean bottle. Cover tightly. May be stored for several months without refrigeration.

Marzipan

Marzipan is actually a paste made of ground blanched almonds and sugar, sometimes with the addition of egg whites. This easy-to-make recipe can be used to cover or fill cakes and pastries, or be shaped into a variety of forms.

Makes about 2 cups

1/3 cup water

3/4 cup sugar

1 cup finely ground blanched almonds

(1) Combine the water and sugar in a small saucepan and cook on medium heat until the mixture reaches 250°F. Do not stir.

(2) Reduce heat, stir in the almonds, and blend well. Continue cooking over low heat, stirring often with a wooden spoon, until the mixture is elastic but not firm.

(3) Transfer the mixture to an oiled work surface and let cool to body temperature, then place in a food processor and grind till paste consistency. If the mixture is too moist, add more finely ground blanched almonds.

(4) Transfer to a covered container and store in the refrigerator for up to 1 week.

Note: For best results, use a candy thermometer to check the temperature of the water-sugar mixture.

Tarts & Tartlets

Learning how to make family-sized tarts and individual tartlets is part of the basic skills every patissière needs to know. Simple to prepare (especially if you freeze pastry-lined pans in advance and just pop them in the oven), tarts and tartlets are also popular and versatile, and come in an astounding variety of savory and sweet flavors.

Tarte Tatin

This classic was created in the 19th century by Stephanie Tatin who, together with her younger sister Caroline, took over the family hotel, Hotel Tatin, after their father died. A moist and luscious upside-down apple cake, Tarte Tatin can be served plain, with Crème Anglaise (Basics page 24), or with fine vanilla ice cream.

Serves 10

3/4 cup butter

1 cup sugar

8 Granny Smith apples, peeled, cored, and cut into quarters

1 recipe Basic Shortcrust Pastry (Basics page 12)

10-inch heat-resistant pie pan (or an ovenproof fry pan)

Large plate to cover pan

(1) In a 10-inch heat-resistant pie pan (or an ovenproof fry pan), melt the butter and sugar and cook over medium heat, stirring occasionally, until golden brown and caramelized.

(2) Remove from heat and set aside to cool for 15 minutes.

(3) Place the apple quarters in the pan in 2 layers of concentric circles.

(4) Return the pan to the heat, reduce to the lowest possible heat, and cook for 1 hour. Check from time to time to make sure that the juices in the pan are gently simmering and not boiling.

(5) Take the pan off the heat and let cool for 15 minutes.

(6) Preheat the oven to 375°F.

(7) Roll out the shortcrust pastry 1/4 inch thick on a lightly floured surface. Drape over the cooked apples, and use a sharp knife to cut the dough to fit the pan. Gather up the excess pieces of dough, make a ball, and cover with plastic wrap. Store in the freezer for future use.

(8) Bake for 25 minutes. Carefully remove from the oven.

(9) Place a large plate over the top of the pan. (The plate should be larger than the pan.) Using oven mitts, hold the pan and plate together on both sides and quickly turn it over. Knock the bottom of the pan and remove it, to reveal a beautiful golden-colored cake. Serve immediately or store for up to 2 days in the refrigerator. Serve warm.

Strawberry Tartlets

These tartlets are a beautiful way to enjoy the finest and freshest strawberries of the season.

Serves 6

1 recipe Basic Shortcrust Pastry (Basics page 12)

2 cups Crème Patissière (Basics page 23)

1 egg, beaten

1 pound small fresh strawberries, hulled

1/4 cup Apricot Glaze (Basics page 27)

2 tablespoons water

6 tartlet pans

Parchment paper

Beans or commercial pie weights

Pastry bag with a 1/3-inch round tip

Small saucepan

(1) Roll out the shortcrust pastry 1/8 inch thick on a lightly floured surface.

(2) Carefully divide the dough among 6 tartlet pans, using your fingers to press the dough into place. Cut off any excess dough around the edges.

(3) Place the pans in the refrigerator for 15 minutes. In the meantime, preheat the oven to 375°F.

(4) Cut out pieces of parchment paper to fit the bottom of the pans, and weigh down with beans or commercial pie weights. Place in the oven and bake for 20 minutes.

(5) Remove the weights and paper. Brush the bottoms and sides with the egg, and bake for an additional 3 minutes. Let cool to room temperature.

(6) Put the pastry cream in a pastry bag with a 1/3-inch round tip. Work from the outside in, piping the cream into the tartlet shells in concentric circles to ensure an even layer.

(7) Working from the outside in, arrange the strawberries, cut side down, evenly over the pastry cream.

(8) In a small saucepan, gently heat the apricot glaze with the water until smooth and syrupy, and brush the strawberries on all sides.

(9) Chill the tartlets for 30 minutes. Serve straight from the refrigerator. Best consumed within 12 hours.

Chocolate Tart

There are many versions of chocolate tarts, but I think this is one of the easiest and simplest to make. For best results, use chocolate with 50% or more cocoa solids.

Serves 10

1 recipe Almond Shortcrust Pastry (Basics page 13)

1 egg, beaten

1 cup whipping cream

10 ounces bittersweet chocolate, cut in small pieces

2 tablespoons brandy or other aromatic liqueur

10-inch tart pan with removable bottom

Parchment paper

Beans or commercial pie weights

Small pan

Double boiler

(1) Roll out the shortcrust pastry 1/8 inch thick on a lightly floured surface.

(2) Carefully transfer the dough to a 10-inch tart pan with removable bottom, pressing it in with your fingers. Cut off any excess dough, roll it into a ball, and wrap tightly in plastic wrap. Store in the freezer for future use.

(3) Place the pan in the refrigerator for 15 minutes. In the meantime, preheat the oven to 375°F.

(4) Cut out a piece of parchment paper to fit the bottom of the pan, and weigh down with beans or commercial pie weights. Place in the oven and bake for 20 minutes.

(5) Remove the weights and paper. Brush the bottom and sides with the egg, and bake for an additional 3 minutes. Let cool to room temperature on a wire rack.

(6) In a small pan, bring the whipping cream to a boil over medium heat.

(7) Remove from heat and add 8 ounces of the chocolate. Stir with a wooden spoon or small whisk until smooth. Blend in the brandy, stirring constantly.

(8) Pour the chocolate mixture into the tart shell and place in the refrigerator uncovered for 1 hour.

(9) Melt the remaining 2 ounces of chocolate in the top of a double boiler until runny.

(10) Turn a baking sheet upside down. Using a spatula, spread the melted chocolate evenly over the baking sheet, until it is the thickness of a butter-knife blade. Refrigerate for 10 minutes, or until the chocolate is firm but not brittle.

(11) Holding a metal spatula with the blade side down at a 45° angle to the sheet, press firmly into the chocolate, pushing steadily forward until a curl forms in the chocolate. Repeat to create enough chocolate curls to cover the top of the cake.

(12) Remove the tart from the refrigerator. Carefully lift the curls with a toothpick or a small skewer, place on the tart, and serve.

Wine-Soaked Pear Tart

This tart requires a little more work than the rest, but once you taste it, you'll know it was worth it.

Serves 10

1 recipe Almond Shortcrust Pastry (Basics page 13)

1 egg, beaten

2 cups dry red wine

1/2 cup sugar

1 cinnamon stick

8 large pears, peeled, cored, and cut in half

1 cup Crème Patissière (Basics page 23)

10-inch tart pan with removable bottom

Parchment paper

Beans or commercial pie weights

Wire rack

Medium saucepan

Pastry bag with a 1/3-inch round tip

(1) Roll out the shortcrust pastry 1/8 inch thick on a lightly floured surface.

(2) Carefully transfer the dough to a 10-inch tart pan with removable bottom, pressing it in with your fingers. Cut off any excess dough, roll it into a ball, and wrap tightly in plastic wrap. Store in the freezer for future use.

(3) Place the pan in the refrigerator for 15 minutes. In the meantime, preheat the oven to 375°F.

(4) Cut out a piece of parchment paper to fit the bottom of the pan, and weigh down with beans or commercial pie weights. Place in the oven and bake for 20 minutes.

(5) Remove the weights and paper. Brush the bottom and sides with the egg, and bake for an additional 3 minutes. Let cool to room temperature on a wire rack.

(6) Combine the wine, sugar, and cinnamon stick in a medium saucepan and bring to a boil.

(7) Add the pear halves, cover, and cook over low heat for 40 minutes. Remove the pears from the liquid with a slotted spoon and transfer to a plate to cool. Continue cooking the wine-sugar mixture on low heat for 15 to 20 minutes, or until it has the consistency of maple syrup. Remove from heat, remove the cinnamon stick, and let cool. (The pears in wine may be prepared 1 day in advance, and stored covered in the refrigerator.)

(8) Put the pastry cream in a pastry bag with a 1/3-inch round tip. Work from the outside in, piping the cream into the tart shell in concentric circles to ensure an even layer.

(9) Arrange the pear halves, cut side down, evenly over the pastry cream.

(10) Brush the pears with the wine-sugar sauce.

(11) Chill the tart for 30 minutes. Serve straight from the refrigerator. Serve within 24 hours.

Blueberry Tartlets

This method can be used with any fresh seasonal berries. It can be baked in a 10-inch tart pan with a removable bottom or in several tartlet pans.

Serves 6

1 recipe Almond Shortcrust Pastry (Basics page 13)

1 egg, beaten

2 cups Crème Patissière (Basics page 23)

1 pound fresh blueberries

1/4 cup Red Currant Glaze (Basics page 28)

2 tablespoons water

6 tartlet pans

Parchment paper

Beans or commercial pie weights

Wire rack

Pastry bag with a 1/3-inch round tip

(1) Roll out the shortcrust pastry 1/8 inch thick on a lightly floured surface.

(2) Carefully divide the dough among the 6 tartlet pans, using your fingers to press the dough into place. Cut off any excess dough around the edges.

(3) Place the pans in the refrigerator for 15 minutes. In the meantime, preheat the oven to 375°F.

(4) Cut out pieces of parchment paper to fit the bottoms of the tartlet pans, and weigh down with beans or commercial pie weights. Place in the oven and bake for 20 minutes.

(5) Remove the weights and paper. Brush the bottoms and sides with the egg, and bake for an additional 3 minutes. Transfer to a wire rack and cool to room temperature.

(6) Put the pastry cream in a pastry bag with a 1/3-inch round tip. Work from the outside in, piping the cream into the tartlet shells in concentric circles to ensure an even layer.

(7) Arrange the blueberries evenly over the pastry cream.

(8) In a small saucepan, gently heat the glaze with 2 tablespoons water until smooth and syrupy, and brush the berries on all sides.

(9) Chill the tarts for 30 minutes. Serve straight from the refrigerator within 12 hours.

Pastéis de Nata

These flaky custard tartlets are everybody's favorite dessert in Portugal. Easy to make, they should be served hot and fresh from the oven.

Makes 20

1/2 recipe Puff Pastry
[Basics page 15]

4 egg yolks

1/2 cup plus 1 tablespoon sugar

1 teaspoon flour

1 1/4 cups sweet cream

2 teaspoons grated lemon zest

1/2 teaspoon cinnamon

3-inch round cutter

Parchment paper

Baking sheet that can fit into your freezer

Medium saucepan

(1) Roll out the shortcrust pastry 1/8 inch thick on a lightly floured surface.

(2) Use a 3-inch round cutter to cut out circles. Gather up the remaining dough, roll out again, and cut out more circles, to create a total of 20 circles.

(3) Place one circle at a time in the palm of your hand and, using your other hand, form it into a little cup. Place the cup on a parchment-lined baking sheet that can fit into your freezer. Repeat with all 20 circles.

(4) Place in the freezer for 15 minutes. In the meantime, preheat the oven to 400°F.

(5) In a medium saucepan, whisk the egg yolks with 1/2 cup of the sugar using a wire whisk. Add the flour gradually, whisking till smooth. Blend in the cream and lemon zest.

(6) Place the saucepan over medium heat and bring to a boil, stirring constantly with the wire whisk. Remove from heat and cool.

(7) When the custard reaches room temperature, pour into the pastry cups. Bake for 15 minutes.

(8) Mix together the remaining tablespoon of sugar with the cinnamon. Sprinkle over the custard cups and serve immediately.

Lemon Tart

This Italian-style tart is traditionally made with the large juicy lemons that grow in the Amalfi region near Naples.

Serves 10

1 recipe Almond Shortcrust
Pastry (Basics page 13)

1 egg, beaten

1 1/4 cups fresh lemon juice

1 tablespoon grated lemon
zest

1 1/2 cups sugar

6 eggs

6 egg yolks

1 cup butter, room
temperature

10-inch tart pan with
removable bottom

Parchment paper

Beans or commercial pie
weights

Small saucepan

(1) Roll out the shortcrust pastry 1/8 inch thick on a lightly floured surface.

(2) Carefully transfer the dough to a 10-inch tart pan with removable bottom, pressing it in with your fingers. Cut off any excess dough, roll it into a ball, and wrap tightly in plastic wrap. Store in the freezer for future use.

(3) Place the pan in the refrigerator for 15 minutes. In the meantime, preheat the oven to 375°F.

(4) Cut out a piece of parchment paper to fit the bottom of the pan, and weigh down with beans or commercial pie weights. Place in the oven and bake for 20 minutes.

(5) Remove the weights and paper. Brush the bottom and sides with the egg, and bake for an additional 3 minutes. Let cool to room temperature on a wire rack. Increase the heat in the oven to 450°F.

(6) In a small saucepan, combine the lemon juice, lemon zest, sugar, eggs, and egg yolks and cook over low heat, whisking constantly, until the sugar has dissolved.

(7) Add 1/2 cup of the butter and continue cooking and whisking until the mixture thickens slightly. Whisk in the remaining 1/2 cup of butter and continuing cooking until the mixture is very thick. Pour into the tart shell.

(8) The oven at this stage should be set to 450°F. Bake for 6 minutes, or until brown spots appear on the top of the lemon cream. Serve warm, or cover with plastic wrap and store in the refrigerator for up to 2 days. Serve chilled.

Errata for page 44.

Pastéis de Catalana

Crema Catalana is a traditional dessert served in many Catalonian homes on St. Joseph's Day. It is so popular that a spiral-shaped iron has been developed to caramelize the sugar for the cream filling. The contrast between the silky cream and the caramelized sugar in these tartlets is simply divine.

Serves 6

1 recipe Almond Shortcrust Pastry (Basics page 13)

1 egg, beaten

1/2 cup cornstarch

4 cups milk

1 cinnamon stick

1 teaspoon grated lemon zest

6 egg yolks

1 1/2 cups sugar

Ice water

6 tartlet pans

Parchment paper

Beans or commercial pie weights

Medium saucepan

Deep bowl

Saucepan

Deep baking pan

(1) Roll out the shortcrust pastry 1/8 inch thick on a lightly floured surface.

(2) Carefully divide the dough among 6 tartlet pans, using your fingers to press the dough into place. Cut off any excess dough around the edges.

(3) Place the pans in the refrigerator for 15 minutes. In the meantime, preheat the oven to 375°F.

(4) Cut out pieces of parchment paper to fit the bottom of the tartlet pans, and weigh down with beans or commercial pie weights. Place in the oven and bake for 20 minutes.

(5) Remove the weights and paper, brush the bottoms and sides with the egg, and bake for an additional 3 minutes. Let cool on a wire rack.

(6) Mix the cornstarch with 1 cup of the milk and set aside.

(7) In a medium saucepan, bring the remaining 3 cups of milk, the cinnamon stick, and the lemon zest to a boil over medium heat, while stirring.

(8) Place the egg yolks in a deep bowl, and whisk in 1 1/4 cups of the sugar until smooth. Whisk in the milk-cornstarch mixture and blend well.

(9) Pour the egg yolk-sugar mixture into a saucepan, whisking gently but constantly. Cook over low heat until the mixture thickens.

(10) Remove from heat and pour through a fine strainer into the prepared tartlet shells. Chill for 1 hour in the refrigerator.

(11) Just before serving, sprinkle the remaining 1/4 cup of sugar evenly over the tartlets. Fill a deep baking pan with ice water and carefully place the tartlet pans inside, taking care not to wet the tartlets. Turn the oven grill on high and place the tartlets close to the heating element for a few seconds—just long enough so that the sugar bubbles and caramelizes. Serve immediately.

Passion Fruit Tart

Exotic and taste-tingling, passion fruit is acquiring more and more fans throughout the world. Prepare the juice by squeezing the pulp from fresh fruit, or use high quality bottled or frozen juice.

Serves 10

1 recipe Almond Shortcrust Pastry [Basics page 13]

1 egg, beaten

4 eggs

3/4 cup sugar

3/4 cup passion fruit juice

1 cup butter, room temperature

10-inch tart pan with removable bottom

Parchment paper

Beans or commercial pie weights

Small bowl

Medium saucepan

(1) Roll out the shortcrust pastry 1/8 inch thick on a lightly floured surface.

(2) Carefully transfer the dough to a 10-inch tart pan with removable bottom, pressing it in with your fingers. Cut off any excess dough, roll it into a ball, and wrap tightly in plastic wrap. Store in the freezer for future use.

(3) Place the pan in the refrigerator for 15 minutes. In the meantime, preheat the oven to 375°F.

(4) Cut out a piece of parchment paper to fit the bottom of the pan, and weigh down with beans or commercial pie weights. Place in the oven and bake for 20 minutes.

(5) Remove the weights and paper. Brush the bottom and sides with the beaten egg, and bake for an additional 3 minutes. Let cool to room temperature on a wire rack. Increase the heat in the oven to 400°F.

(6) In a small bowl, whisk together the 4 eggs and half of the sugar.

(7) In a medium saucepan, bring the passion fruit juice, the remaining sugar, and half of the butter just to the boiling point over low heat, whisking constantly.

(8) Pour the passion fruit mixture into the egg-sugar mixture and blend till smooth. Add the remaining butter and mix well until smooth. Let cool to room temperature and pour into the tart shell.

(9) Bake for 10 minutes. Let cool and store in the refrigerator for up to 2 days. Serve chilled.

Mango and Coconut Cream Tart

The Asian-Pacific influence has reached European shores, and now more than ever, pastry chefs are incorporating those flavors into traditional patisserie. This is one example.

Serves 10

1 recipe Almond Shortcrust Pastry (Basics page 13)

1 egg, beaten

1 1/2 cups canned coconut milk

1/3 cup sugar

4 egg yolks

2 tablespoons cornstarch

1 pound ripe mangoes

1/4 cup Apricot Glaze (Basics page 27)

2 tablespoons water

10-inch tart pan with removable bottom

Parchment paper

Beans or commercial pie weights

Small saucepan

Bowl

Colander

Pastry bag with a 1/3-inch round tip

Small saucepan

(1) Roll out the shortcrust pastry 1/8 inch thick on a lightly floured surface.

(2) Carefully transfer the dough to a 10-inch tart pan with removable bottom, pressing it in with your fingers. Cut off any excess dough, roll it into a ball, and wrap tightly in plastic wrap. Store in the freezer for future use.

(3) Place the pan in the refrigerator for 15 minutes. In the meantime, preheat the oven to 375°F.

(4) Cut out pieces of parchment paper to fit the bottom of the pan, and weigh down with beans or commercial pie weights. Place in the oven and bake for 20 minutes.

(5) Remove the weights and paper. Brush the bottom and sides with the egg, and bake for an additional 3 minutes. Let cool to room temperature on a wire rack.

(6) In a small saucepan, bring the coconut milk and sugar to a boil. In a separate bowl, combine the egg yolks and cornstarch and whisk till smooth.

(7) When the coconut milk boils, lower heat and add the egg yolk-cornstarch mixture. Continue cooking, whisking constantly, for about 3 to 4 minutes, till smooth and thick. Pour the mixture into a clean bowl and let cool to room temperature. Chill thoroughly in the refrigerator for at least 1 hour. (The coconut filling may be prepared up to 1 week in advance, and stored covered in the refrigerator.)

(8) Peel the mangoes and slice thinly. Put them in a colander to drain.

(9) Put the coconut filling in a pastry bag with a 1/3-inch round tip. Work from the outside in, piping the filling into the tart shell in concentric circles to ensure an even layer.

(10) Working from the outside in, arrange the mango slices over the coconut filling in concentric overlapping circles.

(11) In a small saucepan, gently heat the apricot glaze with the water until smooth and syrupy, and brush the mango slices on all sides.

(12) Chill the tart in the refrigerator for 30 minutes. Serve straight from the refrigerator. Best consumed within 12 hours.

Caramelized Banana Tartlets

In this recipe, we'll be using both an unusual flavor combination and a different preparation technique than in previous recipes.

Serves 6

1 recipe Almond Shortcrust Pastry (Basics page 13)

1 egg, beaten

2 cups Crème Patissière (Basics page 23)

6 ripe bananas, cut in 1/8-inch slices

1/3 cup sugar

6 tartlet pans

Parchment paper

Beans or commercial pie weights

Pastry bag with a 1/3-inch round tip

(1) Roll out the shortcrust pastry 1/8 inch thick on a lightly floured surface.

(2) Carefully divide the dough among 6 tartlet pans, using your fingers to press the dough into place. Cut off any excess dough around the edges.

(3) Place the pans in the refrigerator for 15 minutes. In the meantime, preheat the oven to 375°F.

(4) Cut out pieces of parchment paper to fit the bottom of the tartlet pans, and weigh down with beans or commercial pie weights. Place in the oven and bake for 20 minutes.

(5) Remove the weights and paper. Brush the bottoms and sides with the egg, and bake for an additional 3 minutes. Let cool to room temperature.

(6) Put the pastry cream in a pastry bag with a 1/3-inch round tip. Work from the outside in, piping the cream into the tart shell in concentric circles to ensure an even layer.

(7) Working from the outside in, arrange the banana slices over the pastry cream in concentric overlapping circles.

(8) Just before serving, sprinkle the sugar evenly over the tartlets. Fill a deep baking pan with ice water and carefully place the tartlet pans inside, taking care not to wet the tartlets. Turn the oven grill on high and place the tartlets close to the heating element for a few seconds— just long enough so that the sugar bubbles and caramelizes. Serve immediately.

Pineapple Tart

I've always been crazy about pineapples, and love discovering new and interesting ways to serve them. Made with roasted pineapple, this tart is the result of one of my many pineapple experiments—and one of the most successful.

Serves 10

1 recipe Almond Shortcrust Pastry (Basics page 13)

1 egg, beaten

1 1/2 cups passion fruit or other tropical fruit juice

1/4 cup sugar

4 egg yolks

2 tablespoons cornstarch

1 pound fresh pineapple, peeled and cut crosswise into 1/4-inch slices

1/4 cup Apricot Glaze (Basics page 27)

2 tablespoons water

10-inch tart pan with removable bottom

Parchment paper

Beans or commercial pie weights

Small saucepan

Small bowl

Ridged grill pan

Pastry bag with a 1/3-inch round tip

(1) Roll out the shortcrust pastry 1/8 inch thick on a lightly floured surface.

(2) Carefully transfer the dough to a 10-inch tart pan with removable bottom, pressing it in with your fingers. Cut off any excess dough, roll it into a ball, and wrap tightly in plastic wrap. Store in the freezer for future use.

(3) Place the pan in the refrigerator for 15 minutes. In the meantime, preheat the oven to 375°F.

(4) Cut out a piece of parchment paper to fit the bottom of the pan, and weigh down with beans or commercial pie weights. Place in the oven and bake for 20 minutes.

(5) Remove the weights and paper. Brush the bottom and sides with the egg, and bake for an additional 3 minutes. Let cool to room temperature on a wire rack.

(6) In a small saucepan, combine the juice with the sugar and bring to a boil. Lower heat to a simmer.

(7) Whisk together egg yolks and cornstarch in a small bowl. Add to the saucepan, whisking constantly. Continue cooking on low heat for 3 to 4 minutes, till smooth and thick. Pour into a clean bowl and let cool. Cover with plastic wrap and chill thoroughly. (The custard may be prepared up to 1 week in advance, and stored covered in the refrigerator.)

(8) Heat a ridged grill pan on high heat, and sear the pineapple slices till brown grill marks appear. Turn over the pineapple slices and sear on the other side. Set aside to cool.

(9) Put the custard in a pastry bag with a 1/3-inch round tip. Work from the outside in, piping the filling into the tart shell in concentric circles to ensure an even layer.

(10) Working from the outside in, arrange the seared pineapple slices over the custard in concentric overlapping circles.

(11) Gently heat the apricot glaze with the water, stirring until smooth and syrupy. Brush the pineapple slices on all sides.

(12) Chill the tart for 30 minutes. Serve straight from the refrigerator. Serve within 12 hours.

Choux Paste

Choux Paste, also known as choux pastry or Pâte à Choux, is the ultimate classic in European patisserie, and the basis for those éclairs and cream puffs you'll find in every patisserie showcase. It's easy to make with everyday ingredients. Just follow all the instructions carefully and remember not to check the oven until the baking time is over, or your puffs will collapse. Once you've mastered the basic techniques, feel free to create your own shapes and sizes, pipe with your choice of fillings, and enjoy the ecstatic response.

Chocolate Éclairs

These scrumptious éclairs will win you rave reviews. For best results, always use the freshest eggs and finest chocolate for this recipe.

Makes 15

1 recipe Choux Paste (Basics page 16)

1 egg, beaten

3 cups Crème Patissière (Basics page 23)

3 ounces bittersweet chocolate, cut in small pieces

1 tablespoon heavy cream

1 tablespoon butter, room temperature

Baking sheet

Pastry bag with a 1/3-inch round tip

Bowl

Double boiler

Parchment paper

Small saucepan

(1) Preheat the oven to 375°F. Grease a baking sheet.

(2) Place the choux pastry in a pastry bag with a 1/3-inch round tip. Pipe 4-inch strips onto the baking sheet, leaving about 1/2 inch between each strip.

(3) Brush the strips with the beaten egg and bake for 25 minutes, or until golden brown. Remove from the baking sheet and let cool on a wire rack.

(4) In a bowl, mix the pastry cream until smooth and transfer to a pastry bag with a 1/3-inch round tip.

(5) Hold one of the éclairs in the palm of your hand, with the side that touched the baking sheet facing up. Stick the tip in close to the bottom edge and pipe in the filling just until the éclair feels substantially heavier. Repeat with the other éclairs.

(6) Heat the chocolate in the top of a double boiler until melted. Remove from heat and add the heavy cream and butter. Mix well.

(7) Lightly dip the top side of the éclair (the egg-brushed side) in the chocolate mixture. With the chocolate side facing up, place on a tray lined with parchment paper and put in the refrigerator. Chill for 30 minutes and serve, or store in the refrigerator for up to 2 days.

For variation: Double Chocolate Éclairs
Real chocolate lovers can prepare a chocolate-filled Chocolate Éclair by replacing Step 4 with the following:
1/4 cup heavy cream
3 ounces bittersweet chocolate, cut in small pieces
3 cups Crème Patissière

Pour the heavy cream into a small saucepan and bring just to the boiling point. Place the chocolate in a bowl and pour the cream over. Mix well and let cool to room temperature.
Add the pastry cream and mix until smooth. Cover and chill for 1 hour in the refrigerator. Transfer to a pastry bag with a 1/3-inch round tip.

Caramel Éclairs

The caramel sauce that tops these luscious éclairs is a little different from the one you'll find in commercial bakeries. I find this pure and rich natural version to be far superior.

Makes 15

1 recipe Choux Paste (Basics page 16)

1 egg, beaten

1/2 cup sugar

1 tablespoon water

1 cup heavy cream

1 1/2 cups Crème Patissière (Basics page 23)

Baking sheet

Pastry bag with a 1/3-inch round tip

Small saucepan

Medium bowl

Parchment paper

(1) Preheat the oven to 375°F. Grease a baking sheet.

(2) Place the choux pastry in a pastry bag with a 1/3-inch round tip. Pipe 4-inch long strips onto the baking sheet, leaving about 1/2 inch between each strip.

(3) Brush the strips with the beaten egg and bake for 25 minutes, or until golden brown. Remove from the baking sheet and let cool on a wire rack.

(4) In the meantime, combine the sugar and water in a small saucepan, and cook over medium heat until light brown and caramelized. Do not stir.

(5) Pour in the heavy cream and cook, stirring constantly, until the sauce thickens. Let cool to room temperature.

(6) In a medium bowl, use a wire hand whisk to whisk the pastry cream and 1/2 cup of the caramel sauce together till smooth. Cover and chill for 1 hour.

(7) Transfer the mixture to a pastry bag with a 1/3-inch round tip.

(8) Hold one of the éclairs in the palm of your hand, with the side that touched the baking sheet facing up. Stick the tip in close to the bottom edge and pipe the filling in just until the éclair feels substantially heavier. Repeat with the other éclairs (see page 57).

(9) Lightly dip the top side of the éclair (the egg-brushed side) in the remaining caramel sauce. With the caramel side facing up, place on a tray lined with parchment paper and put in the refrigerator. Chill for 30 minutes and serve, or store in the refrigerator for up to 2 days.

Vanilla Cream Puffs

These sinfully rich cream puffs are guaranteed to satisfy any sweet tooth. For a cool treat on a hot summer's day, substitute premium vanilla ice cream for the cream filling. Serve with chocolate sauce for a truly decadent dessert.

Makes 15

1 recipe Choux Paste (Basics page 16)

1 egg, beaten

1 cup whipping cream

1/2 teaspoon pure vanilla extract

3/4 cup sugar

2 cups Crème Patissière (Basics page 23)

1 tablespoon water

1 tablespoon fresh lemon juice

Baking sheet

Pastry bag with a 1/3-inch round tip

Electric mixer

Medium bowl

Pastry bag with a 1/3-inch open star tip

Parchment paper

Tray that fits into your refrigerator

Small saucepan

(1) Preheat the oven to 375°F. Grease a baking sheet.

(2) Place the choux pastry in a pastry bag with a 1/3-inch round tip. Pipe 2-inch filled circles onto the baking sheet, leaving about 1 inch between each circle.

(3) Brush the circles with the beaten egg and bake for 25 minutes, or until golden brown. Remove from the baking sheet and let cool on a wire rack.

(4) Place the whipping cream, vanilla, and 1/4 cup of the sugar into the bowl of an electric mixer and whip till stiff.

(5) In a medium bowl, use a hand whisk to whisk the pastry cream and whipped cream together till smooth. Cover and chill for 1 hour.

(6) Transfer the mixture to a pastry bag with a 1/3-inch open star tip.

(7) Hold one of the cream puffs in the palm of your hand, with the side that touched the baking sheet facing up. Stick the tip in just under one of the bottom edges and pipe in the filling just until the cream puff feels substantially heavier. Repeat with the other cream puffs. Place on a parchment-lined baking sheet that fits into your refrigerator, and chill for 30 minutes.

(8) In a small saucepan, combine the remaining 1/2 cup sugar, water, and lemon juice and cook over medium heat, stirring occasionally, until the mixture is light brown and caramelized.

(9) Remove the puffs from the refrigerator and lightly dip the top side (the egg-brushed side) of each in the caramel sauce. With the caramel side facing up, place on the tray and return to the refrigerator. Chill for 30 minutes and serve, or store in the refrigerator for up to 2 days.

Hazelnut Cream Puffs

An exquisite blend of textures and flavors, this hazelnut-walnut cream puff with its caramel topping is to die for.

Makes 15

1 recipe Choux Paste (Basics page 16)

1 egg, beaten

1/2 cup Nutella or other nut spread

2 cups Crème Patissière (Basics page 23)

1/2 cup coarsely chopped toasted walnuts

1/2 cup sugar

1 tablespoon water

1 tablespoon fresh lemon juice

Baking sheet

Pastry bag with a 1/3-inch round tip

Medium bowl

Pastry bag with a 1/3-inch open star tip

Tray that fits into your refrigerator

Small saucepan

(1) Preheat the oven to 375°F. Grease a baking sheet.

(2) Place the choux pastry in a pastry bag with a 1/3-inch round tip. Pipe 2-inch filled circles onto the baking sheet, leaving about 1 inch between each circle.

(3) Brush the circles with the beaten egg and bake for 25 minutes, or until golden brown. Remove from the baking sheet and let cool on a wire rack.

(4) In a medium bowl, use a hand whisk to whisk the Nutella, pastry cream, and walnuts together till smooth. Cover and chill for 1 hour.

(5) Transfer the mixture to a pastry bag with a 1/3-inch open star tip.

(6) Hold one of the cream puffs in the palm of your hand, with the side that touched the baking sheet facing up. Stick the tip in just under one of the bottom edges and pipe in the filling just until the cream puff feels substantially heavier. Repeat with the other cream puffs. Place on a tray that can fit into your refrigerator, and chill for 30 minutes.

(7) In a small saucepan, combine the sugar, water, and lemon juice and cook over medium heat, stirring occasionally, until the mixture is light brown and caramelized.

(8) Remove the puffs from the refrigerator and lightly dip the topside (the egg-brushed side) of each puff in the caramel sauce. With the caramel side facing up, place on a tray and return to the refrigerator. Chill for 30 minutes and serve, or store in the refrigerator for up to 2 days.

Chocolate Coconut Cream Puffs

Coconut milk and a toasted coconut topping add a tropical twist to these cream puffs, an exotic touch to a traditional favorite.

Makes 15

1 recipe Choux Paste (Basics page 16)

1 egg, beaten

1 1/2 cups whipping cream

1 recipe Chocolate Ganache (Basics page 22)

1/2 cup coconut milk

6 ounces bittersweet chocolate, cut into pieces

1/2 cup toasted coconut flakes, for garnish

Baking sheet

Pastry bag with a 1/3-inch round tip

Electric mixer

Large bowl

Parchment paper

Tray that fits in your refrigerator

Double boiler

(1) Preheat the oven to 375°F. Grease a baking sheet.

(2) Place the choux pastry in a pastry bag with a 1/3-inch round tip. Pipe 2-inch filled circles onto the baking sheet, leaving about 1 inch between each circle.

(3) Brush the circles with the beaten egg and bake for 25 minutes, or until golden brown. Remove from the baking sheet and let cool on a wire rack.

(4) Place 1 cup of the whipping cream in the bowl of an electric mixer and whip till soft and foamy. Place in the refrigerator for 1 hour.

(5) In a large bowl, beat together the chocolate ganache and the coconut milk until smooth and uniform. Using a rubber spatula, fold in the chilled whipped cream until blended.

(6) Transfer the mixture to a pastry bag with a 1/3-inch round tip.

(7) Hold one of the cream puffs in the palm of your hand, with the side that touched the baking sheet facing up. Stick the tip in just under one of the bottom edges and pipe in the filling just until the cream puff feels substantially heavier. Repeat with the other cream puffs. Place on a tray lined with parchment and place in the refrigerator for 30 minutes.

(8) Melt the chocolate in the top of a double boiler over low heat. Remove from the heat and, using a rubber spatula, fold in the remaining 1/2 cup of whipping cream until blended.

(9) Remove the puffs from the refrigerator and lightly dip the top side (the egg-brushed side) of each in the chocolate sauce. Place the dipped puffs on the tray, with the chocolate side facing up. Sprinkle the coconut flakes over top and return to the refrigerator. Chill for 30 minutes and serve, or store in the refrigerator for up to 2 days.

Paris-Brest

Like the bagel inspired by a horse's stirrup, the Paris-Brest was inspired by a bicycle wheel. A ring-shaped pastry filled with cream and sprinkled with almonds and confectioner's sugar, it was invented in 1891 by a Parisian pastry chef whose patisserie was along the route of the bicycle race from Paris to Brest, in honor of the cyclists. In 1903, this race was renamed the Tour de France.

Makes 10

1 recipe Choux Paste (Basics page 16)

1 egg, beaten

1/4 cup toasted sliced almonds

1 cup butter, room temperature

1/4 cup Nutella or other nut spread

2 tablespoons confectioner's sugar

2 baking sheets

Pastry bag with a 1/3-inch round tip

Electric mixer

Pastry bag with a 1/3-inch open star tip

(1) Preheat the oven to 375°F. Grease 2 baking sheets.

(2) Place the choux pastry in a pastry bag with a 1/3-inch round tip. Pipe a 5-inch ring of dough onto one of the baking sheets. Pipe another ring inside the first. Repeat to make 10 double rings.

(3) On each of the 10 double rings, pipe a third ring of choux pastry in the ridge between the first two rings.

(4) Brush the rings with the beaten egg and sprinkle with the almonds. Bake for 25 minutes, or until golden brown.

(5) In the meantime, place the butter and Nutella in the bowl of an electric mixer and beat till light and fluffy. Cover and chill in the refrigerator for 30 minutes.

(6) When the rings have finished baking, carefully transfer them to a wire rack and cool to room temperature.

(7) Working quickly with a sharp knife, slice the rings in half horizontally to make two layers, making sure that the top and bottom layer are of equal width.

(8) Place the chilled nut cream in a pastry bag with a 1/3-inch open star tip, and pipe generous dots of filling, one next to another, on the bottom piece of each pastry ring. Place the upper piece on top. The result should look like a sandwich.

(9) Chill in the refrigerator for 30 minutes, or up to 24 hours. Remove 30 minutes before serving and dust with confectioner's sugar passed through a fine strainer.

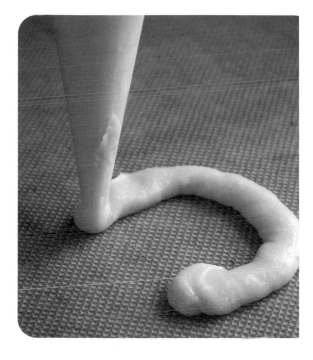

Saint-Honoré

Named for the patron saint of pastry bakers, this traditional dessert combines choux pastry, shortcrust pastry, caramel, and enriched pastry cream for an absolutely sinful treat.

Makes 10

1/2 recipe Basic Shortcrust Pastry (Basics page 12)

1 recipe Choux Paste (Basics page 16)

1 egg, beaten

2 cups whipping cream

1/2 teaspoon pure vanilla extract

3/4 cup sugar

1 cup Crème Patissière (Basics page 23)

1 tablespoon water

1 tablespoon fresh lemon juice

3 baking sheets

Parchment paper

4-inch round cutter

Pastry bag with a 1/3-inch round tip

Electric mixer

Small saucepan

Pastry bag with a Saint-Honoré tip

(1) Preheat the oven to 375°F. Grease 2 baking sheets. Line a third baking sheet with parchment paper.

(2) Roll out the shortcrust pastry 1/8 inch thick and cut out 12 circles using a 4-inch round cutter. Place the circles on the parchment paper-lined baking sheet and set aside.

(3) Place the choux pastry in a pastry bag with a 1/3-inch round tip. Pipe thirty 1-inch filled circles onto the 2 greased baking sheets, leaving about 1/2 inch between each circle. Brush the choux pastry circles with the beaten egg, and bake for 25 minutes, or until golden brown. Remove from the baking sheet and place on a wire rack to cool.

(5) Brush the shortcrust pastry with the remaining beaten egg and bake for 15 minutes, or until golden brown. Place on a wire rack to cool.

(6) Place the whipping cream, vanilla, and 1/4 cup of the sugar into the bowl of an electric mixer and whip till stiff.

(7) Use a wire whisk to blend the whipped cream with the pastry cream till smooth. Cover and chill in the refrigerator for 1 hour. Transfer half of the pastry cream mixture to a pastry bag with a 1/3-inch round tip.

(8) Hold one of the cream puffs in the palm of your hand, with the side that touched the baking sheet facing up. Stick the tip in just under the bottom edge and pipe in the filling just until it feels substantially heavier in your hand. Repeat with the other cream puffs.

(9) In a small saucepan, combine the remaining 1/2 cup sugar, water, and lemon juice and cook over medium heat, stirring occasionally, until the mixture is light brown and caramelized.

(10) Lightly dip the bottom of one cream puff in the caramel and stick it onto the edge of one of the shortcrust pastry circles. Follow the same technique to stick two more cream puffs on the pastry circle to form a triangle. Leave the center of the pastry circle free. Repeat with the other cream puffs and pastry circles.

(11) Place the remaining half of the pastry cream mixture in a pastry bag with a Saint-Honoré tip. Pipe strips of filling between the cream puffs and into the center of each pastry circle, and between the cream puffs. Chill for 30 minutes and serve, or store up to 24 hours in the refrigerator.

Easy & Elegant Cakes

Having a freshly baked cake around the house always lifts my spirits, and certainly those of friends who just happen to drop by on a rainy day. The cakes you'll find in this chapter are particularly easy to make, even for busy people with no patience for long and complicated recipes.

Before you begin, please remember: The quality of the raw materials used directly affects the final product. Use only the freshest produce, like ripe — but not overripe—fruit, and pay attention to details. Even the quality of liqueur you use can mean the difference between ordinary and exceptional flavor in your finished cake.

You'll notice that several of the recipes below call for 3-inch parchment paper or aluminum baking cups, which are generally used for muffins or cupcakes. Parchment paper cups are the best, as they are the closest and easiest way to approximate the individual serving cakes sold in traditional French patisseries. If you prefer, feel free to use mini-kugelhof or mini-loaf pans instead, just remember to fill them only 2/3 full, unless otherwise indicated, to allow room for the cake to rise. You may also use larger pans if desired, but remember that the larger the pan, the longer the baking time.

Coffee Muffins

Using high quality, freshly brewed coffee or espresso in this recipe will produce a more flavorful and aromatic muffin. Served with a glass of orange juice or a cup of coffee, it makes a satisfying (and refreshing) midmorning snack.

Makes 12

4 eggs

1 1/2 cups sugar

1 cup melted butter

1/2 cup prepared coffee or espresso

2 cups all-purpose flour

1 tablespoon baking powder

1/2 cup ground almonds

2 tablespoons Amaretto

2 tablespoons coffee liqueur

12-cup muffin pan, or nonstick muffin pan

Electric mixer

(1)   Preheat the oven to 375°F. Grease a 12-cup muffin pan, or use a nonstick muffin pan, and set aside.

(2)   In the bowl of an electric mixer, using the wire whisk attachment, beat the eggs and sugar on high till soft and foamy.

(3)   Reduce the speed to medium and, with the machine running, add the butter and coffee. Beat until the mixture is smooth.

(4)   Reduce to low speed and gradually add the flour, baking powder, and almonds. Continue to beat until smooth.

(5)   Add the Amaretto and coffee liqueur, and mix until smooth.

(6)   Distribute the batter evenly between the muffin cups, making sure that each cup is about 2/3 full. Fill any empty muffin cups with a little water and bake for 15 minutes, or until a toothpick inserted in the center comes out clean. Transfer to a wire rack to cool. Store in a covered container at room temperature for up to 2 days.

English Lemon Tea Cakes

This is a traditional English cake. You're likely to find it served along with a pot of steaming tea, scones, clotted cream, and cucumber sandwiches at a typical High Tea in the British Isles.

Makes 12

3 eggs

3/4 cup sugar

2 tablespoons fresh lemon juice

2 teaspoons grated lemon zest

1 1/4 cups unbleached all-purpose flour

1 teaspoon baking powder

3/4 cup melted butter

1/4 cup Apricot Glaze (Basics page 27)

1/4 cup water

Twelve 3-inch brioche pans

Large bowl

Baking sheet

(1) Preheat the oven to 375°F. Grease twelve 3-inch brioche pans.

(2) Combine the eggs and sugar in a large bowl and whisk with a wire whisk until smooth.

(3) Blend in the lemon juice and lemon zest.

(4) Fold in the flour and baking powder with a spatula. Mix gently till smooth.

(5) Fold in the melted butter. Cover the bowl and let rest at room temperature for 20 minutes.

(6) Fill each brioche pan 2/3 full with the batter.

(7) Place the pans on a baking sheet and bake for 25 minutes, or until a toothpick inserted in the center of each cake comes out clean. Transfer the cakes to a wire rack to cool.

(8) In the meantime, heat the apricot glaze and water almost to the boiling point. Remove from heat and brush the tops of the cakes. Set aside to dry. Store in an airtight container at room temperature for up to 2 days.

Individual Banana Cakes

Especially good with a pot of blended herbal tea, these cakes are distinguished from traditional banana bread by their light texture yet deep banana flavor. Use very ripe (but not overripe) bananas.

Makes 12

3/4 cup butter

1 egg

1/2 cup confectioner's sugar

1 cup unbleached all-purpose flour

1 teaspoon baking powder

Pinch salt

1 1/4 cups ripe mashed bananas

2 tablespoons raisins

1/2 teaspoon grated lemon zest

1/4 cup coarsely chopped pecans

Twelve 3-inch parchment paper or aluminum baking cups

Baking tray

Large bowl

(1) Preheat the oven to 375°F. Place twelve 3-inch parchment paper or aluminum baking cups on a baking tray and set aside.

(2) Combine the butter, egg, and confectioner's sugar in a large bowl till smooth.

(3) Mix in the flour, baking powder, salt, bananas, raisins, and lemon zest and blend well. Stir in the pecans.

(4) Cover the bowl, and set aside at room temperature for 20 minutes.

(5) Transfer the batter to the baking cups and fill each 2/3 full.

(6) Bake for 25 minutes, or until a toothpick inserted in the center of each cake comes out clean. Let cool on a wire rack. Store in an airtight container at room temperature for up to 2 days.

Chocolate Fondant

Served hot, this wickedly rich chocolate cake is crispy on the outside with a luscious creamy center. It's no wonder that it's become one of the restaurant world's most popular desserts.

Makes 6

3 eggs, separated

1/2 cup sugar

4 ounces chocolate, cut in small pieces

1/3 cup butter

1 tablespoon cocoa

2 tablespoons flour

Confectioner's sugar, for garnish

6-cup muffin pan with baking cups

Electric mixer

Bowl

Double boiler

(1) Preheat the oven to 375°F. Line a 6-cup muffin pan with baking cups.

(2) In the bowl of an electric mixer and using the wire whisk, beat the egg whites with 1/4 cup of the sugar until stiff.

(3) In a separate bowl, whip the egg yolks with the remaining sugar until fluffy and smooth.

(4) Melt the chocolate, butter, and cocoa in the top of a double boiler.

(5) Using a rubber spatula, combine all three mixtures together till smooth. Fold in the flour gradually.

(6) Pour the batter into the baking cups and bake for 12 minutes. Sprinkle with confectioner's sugar and serve immediately.

Note: You can make the batter in advance and keep it for up to 48 hours in the refrigerator before baking.

Financiers

Financiers, made in all different sizes, are one of the most popular cakes in France. You'll find tiny ones served with coffee at the end of a meal in elite restaurants, and all kinds of renditions in neighborhood patisseries.

Makes 6

1/2 cup butter

5 egg whites

1/2 cup ground blanched almonds

1 cup confectioner's sugar

1/2 cup unbleached all-purpose flour

1 tablespoon coffee, caramel, raspberry, or blueberry flavoring, optional

Six 3-inch parchment paper or aluminum baking cups

Baking sheet

Heavy frying pan

Medium bowl

(1) Preheat the oven to 375°F. Place six 3-inch parchment paper or aluminum baking cups on a baking sheet and set aside.

(2) Melt the butter in a heavy frying pan over high heat. Continue to cook until the sizzling sound stops and the butter is a light hazelnut hue. Remove from heat.

(3) In a medium bowl, combine the egg whites, almonds, confectioner's sugar, and flour, and beat with a wire whisk till smooth.

(4) Pour in the browned butter and blend well. This mixture is the basis of the Financiers cake. At this point, you can add the flavoring of your choice, adding 1/2 tablespoon at a time, and tasting after each addition. Whatever you add, make sure it doesn't dominate the delicate flavor and color of the batter.

(5) Spoon the mixture into the baking cups, filling each 3/4 full.

(6) Bake for 20 minutes, or until a toothpick inserted in the center comes out clean. Transfer to a wire rack to cool. Store in a covered container at room temperature for up to 2 days.

Honey Cake

This cake hails from the Jewish kitchen, and is traditionally served on Rosh Hashanah, the Jewish New Year.

Makes 6

1 cup honey

1 egg

1/4 cup milk

1 teaspoon grated orange zest

1 tablespoon brandy

1 cup unbleached all-purpose flour

1 teaspoon baking powder

Six 3-inch parchment paper or aluminum baking cups

Baking sheet

Small saucepan

Bowl

(1) Preheat the oven to 375°F. Place six 3-inch parchment paper or aluminum baking cups on a baking sheet and set aside.

(2) Pour the honey into a small saucepan and heat gently until it is a thin syrup. Do not boil.

(3) Whisk together the egg, milk, orange zest, and brandy in a bowl till smooth.

(4) Pour in the honey, flour, and baking powder and beat with a wire whisk till well blended. Cover the bowl with plastic wrap and set aside for 20 minutes.

(5) Spoon the mixture into the cups, filling each 2/3 full.

(6) Bake for 25 minutes, or until a toothpick inserted in the center comes out clean. Transfer to a wire rack to cool. Store in a covered container at room temperature for up to 2 days.

Torta di Mele alle Mandorle

Native to Florence, this traditional cake is popular throughout Tuscany. For best results, make sure that you select flavorful ripe apples.

Serves 12–14

2 tablespoons butter

6 tablespoons sugar

2 Golden Delicious apples, peeled, cored, and thinly sliced

2 tablespoons fresh lemon juice

2 teaspoons grated lemon zest

3/4 cup ground blanched almonds

2 tablespoons unbleached all-purpose flour

1/2 cup milk

4 eggs

1/3 cup confectioner's sugar, for garnish

8 x 3-inch loaf pan

Bowl

Food processor

(1) Preheat the oven to 375°F. Grease a 8 x 3-inch loaf pan with the butter, sprinkle with 2 tablespoons of the sugar, and set aside.

(2) Place the apple slices in a bowl with the lemon juice.

(3) Combine the lemon zest, almonds, remaining 4 tablespoons sugar, and flour in the bowl of a food processor and process with the metal blade until the almonds are ground to flour consistency.

(4) Add the milk and eggs and process till the mixture is smooth, with a butter-like consistency.

(5) Pour the batter into the bowl with the apples and mix well, until all the apple slices are covered with the mixture. Transfer to the loaf pan and bake for 35 minutes. Cool slightly on a wire rack, cut into 3-inch squares, and sprinkle with confectioner's sugar. Serve warm or at room temperature.

Bolo Ensopado em Vinho do Porto

This is my version the Portuguese-style cake soaked in port, a simple but marvelous cake that we enjoy.

Makes 9

1 cup sugar

1/2 cup butter, room temperature

3 eggs

3/4 cup unbleached all-purpose flour

1 teaspoon baking powder

1 cup water

1 cup sugar

1/4 cup good quality port wine

1/2 cup whipping cream

12-cup muffin pan, or non-stick muffin pan

Electric mixer

Small saucepan

Electric mixer

Serving platter with raised edges

Pastry bag with a 1/4- inch open star tip

(1) Preheat the oven to 375°F. Grease a 12-cup muffin pan, or use a nonstick muffin pan, and set aside.

(2) Combine the sugar and butter in the bowl of an electric mixer and whip with the wire whisk till white and creamy.

(3) With the machine running, add the eggs and continue whipping until fluffy.

(4) Gradually fold in the flour and baking powder with a rubber spatula.

(5) Distribute the batter evenly between 9 muffin cups. Fill the empty muffin cups with a little water and bake for 15 minutes, or until a toothpick inserted in the center comes out clean.

(6) In the meantime, mix the water and sugar in a small saucepan and bring to a boil. Do not stir. Remove from heat and stir in the port wine.

(7) Remove the cakes from the muffin pan and place on a serving platter with raised edges. Pour the syrup over the cakes and let stand 30 minutes at room temperature.

(8) Cover and chill in the refrigerator for 1 hour, or store for up to 2 days in the refrigerator. Before serving place the whipping cream in the bowl of an electric mixer and beat untill stiff. Transfer to a pastry bag with a 1/4- inch open star tip and pipe small buds on top of each cake.

Mini Almond Orange Cakes

Baked in five individual 4-inch kugelhof pans or a family-sized 8-inch kugelhof pan, this is a perfect winter cake. It's easy to put together and fills the house with a tempting fragrance while it bakes.

Serves 5

3/4 cup candied orange peel

1 tablespoon orange liqueur (Cointreau or Grand Marnier)

3/4 cup butter, room temperature

1/2 teaspoon salt

3/4 cup confectioner's sugar

3 eggs

1/2 cup fresh orange juice

2 teaspoons grated orange zest

1 1/4 cups unbleached all-purpose flour

1/2 cup ground blanched almonds

1 teaspoon baking powder

Five 4-inch kugelhopf pans, or one 8-inch kugelhopf pan

Electric mixer

(1) Preheat the oven to 375°F. Grease five 4-inch kugelhopf pans, or one 8-inch kugelhof pan.

(2) Macerate the candied orange peel in the liqueur for 1 hour at room temperature.

(3) Combine the butter, salt, confectioner's sugar, and eggs in the bowl of an electric mixer. Use the wire whisk attachment to whisk together till light and smooth.

(4) Blend in the orange juice and orange zest.

(5) Transfer the mixture to a larger bowl, if necessary, and fold in the flour, almonds, baking powder, and macerated orange peels. Set aside 15 peels, for garnish.

(6) Cover the batter with plastic wrap and place in the refrigerator to rest for 2 hours.

(7) If using 4-inch kugelhopf pans, place 3 orange peels inside each pan and fill 3/4 full with batter. Bake for 25 minutes, or until golden brown. Transfer to a wire rack and cool for 10 minutes before removing from the pans. If using an 8-inch kugelhopf pan, place all the orange peels inside, fill 3/4 full with batter, and bake for 35 minutes, or until golden brown. Let cool 15 minutes on the wire rack before removing from the pan.

(8) Cool fully before serving, or store in an airtight container at room temperature for up to 2 days.

PETITS FOURS

Petits fours are elaborately decorated bite-sized cakes that are usually served at the end of a meal. They are also wonderful with coffee or tea on special occasions. Best made and served the same day, petits fours require more complicated techniques, but the joy they bring makes it worth the effort.

Caramel Hazelnut Shortbread

These Swiss petits fours have a unique taste and consistency. For best results, follow the recipe exactly, step by step.

Makes 25

1 recipe Almond Shortcrust Pastry (Basics page 13), with added cocoa

2 tablespoons water

1/4 cup glucose

3/4 cup sugar

1/2 cup whipping cream

2 tablespoons butter

1/2 cup coarsely chopped hazelnuts

Small saucepan

Baking sheet

Parchment paper

1-inch round cutter

(1) Prepare the shortcrust pastry, wrap in plastic wrap, and chill in the refrigerator for 30 minutes.

(2) In the meantime, combine the water, glucose, and sugar in a small saucepan and cook, stirring constantly, over medium heat for about 10 minutes, until the mixture turns dark brown and caramelizes.

(3) Lower heat and stir in the whipping cream and butter. Cook while stirring until the sauce is very thick.

(4) Add the hazelnuts, mix well, and cook 5 minutes.

(5) Pour the mixture out onto a greased baking sheet and let cool completely.

(6) Preheat the oven to 375°F. Line a baking sheet with parchment paper.

(7) Remove the dough from the refrigerator and roll out 1/8 inch thick on a lightly floured surface.

(8) Use a 1-inch round cutter to cut out circles. Gather up the remaining dough, roll out, and cut additional circles, for a total of 25 circles. Place on the parchment-lined baking sheet.

(9) Bake for 12 minutes. Remove and place on a wire rack to cool.

(10) Place a teaspoon of the caramel-nut mixture in the center of each cookie. Do not flatten.

(11) Transfer the cookies to the freezer for 10 minutes and serve. May be kept at room temperature in an airtight jar for 24 hours.

Cigarettes

These are also considered tuiles, although they are more delicate than other tuiles. Traditionally, they are served at the end of a meal with a glass of good brandy or grappa.

Makes 15

4 egg whites

1/2 cup confectioner's sugar

1/3 cup melted butter

3/4 cup unbleached all-purpose flour

Large bowl

Baking sheet

Silicone baking sheet

(1) In a large bowl, combine the egg whites and confectioner's sugar and whisk together till smooth.

(2) Gradually blend in the melted butter and then the flour. Cover with plastic wrap and chill in the refrigerator for 30 minutes.

(3) Preheat the oven to 375°F. Line a baking sheet with a silicone baking sheet.

(4) Using a tablespoon, drop tablespoons of the mixture onto the baking sheet, about 3 inches apart. Use the back of the spoon to flatten the cookies into 2-inch circles.

(5) Bake for 10 minutes.

(6) Remove from the oven and, while the cookies are still warm, use a palette knife to remove one tuile at a time and wrap it around the handle of a wooden spoon, like a cigarette or cigar. Cool for 10 minutes on the spoon. Repeat with the remaining tuiles. If you have several wooden spoons, you can make a few cigarettes at the same time. If not, return the tuiles to the oven for a few seconds before wrapping around the spoon.

(7) Serve within 12 hours after baking.

Almond Tuiles

Although I've made this recipe hundreds of times, the fact that I can bend the cookies into so many different types of shapes while they are warm still fills me with delight.

Makes 15

1 egg

2 egg whites

1/2 cup sugar

3/4 cup sliced blanched almonds

1/4 cup unbleached all-purpose flour

Large bowl

Baking sheet

Silicone baking sheet

(1) In a large bowl, combine the egg, egg whites, and sugar and whisk together with a wire whisk. Add the almonds and mix till smooth.

(2) Cover with plastic wrap and chill in the refrigerator for 30 minutes.

(3) Preheat the oven to 375°F. Line a baking sheet with a silicone baking sheet.

(4) Remove the mixture from the refrigerator and add the flour. Blend till smooth.

(5) Using a tablespoon, drop heaping tablespoons of the mixture on the baking sheet, about 3 inches apart. Use the back of the spoon to flatten the cookies into 2-inch circles. Depending on the size of your baking sheet, you may have to make the cookies in 2 batches.

(6) Bake for 10 minutes.

(7) Remove from the oven and, working quickly, remove the cookies, one at a time, from the baking sheet with a thin spatula. Drape each cookie over a rolling pin to create a curved shape. If the cookies become too brittle to curve on the rolling pin, return the baking sheet to the warm oven for a few seconds to soften.

(8) Cool cookies for 10 minutes on the rolling pin, then carefully transfer to an airtight container. Best consumed within 12 hours after baking.

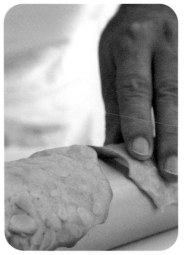

Chocolate Tuiles

These tuiles have a special taste and texture, achieved by careful baking. To know when they are ready, touch the center of each circle to make sure it is dry and not sticky, or else it will fall apart.

Makes 15

1/4 cup fresh orange juice

2 egg whites

1/2 cup confectioner's sugar

1/4 cup melted butter

1 tablespoon unbleached all-purpose flour

1 tablespoon cocoa

1/4 cup grated bittersweet chocolate

1/4 cup ground blanched almonds

Baking sheet

Silicone baking sheet

Large bowl

(1) Preheat the oven to 375°F. Line a baking sheet with a silicone baking sheet.

(2) In a large bowl, combine the orange juice, egg whites, confectioner's sugar, and melted butter. Beat with a wire whisk until smooth.

(3) Add the flour, cocoa, and chocolate and mix well. Stir in the almonds and mix till smooth.

(4) Using a tablespoon, drop heaping tablespoons of the mixture onto the baking sheet, about 3 inches apart. Use the back of the spoon to flatten the cookies into 2-inch circles. Depending on the size of your baking sheet, you may have to make the cookies in 2 batches.

(5) Bake for 10 minutes or until the center of each cookie is dry.

(6) Remove from the oven and, working quickly, remove the cookies, one at a time, from the baking sheet with a thin spatula. Drape each cookie over a rolling pin to create a curved shape. If the cookies become too brittle to form on the rolling pin, soften by returning the baking sheet to the oven for a few seconds.

(7) Cool cookies for 10 minutes on the rolling pin, then carefully transfer to an airtight container. Best consumed within 12 hours after baking.

Hazelnut Cream Cones

Although this recipe takes time to prepare, it makes one of the most unusual, pretty, and delicious petits fours you've ever tasted.

Makes 12

1 recipe Cigarettes (Petits Fours page 87)

1 recipe Marzipan (Basics page 30)

1/4 cup Nutella or other nut spread

1 tablespoon Amaretto

5 ounces bittersweet chocolate, cut in small pieces

12 whole hazelnuts, for garnish

Medium bowl

Pastry bag with a 1/3-inch round tip

Baking sheet that fits in your freezer

Double boiler

(1) Prepare the cigarette dough and bake according to the recipe directions. Use oven mitts to form each cigarette into the shape of an ice cream cone. Place seam side down on a work surface and let cool for 10 minutes.

(2) In a medium bowl, combine the marzipan, Nutella, and Amaretto, and mix with a hand whisk till smooth. Transfer to a pastry bag with a 1/3-inch round tip and fill each cone 3/4 full.

(3) Place the filled cones on a baking sheet that fits in your freezer. Place in the freezer for 20 minutes. At this point, the cones may be frozen for up to 1 week. If the cones have been frozen for more than 20 minutes, let them defrost for 30 minutes before proceeding to the next step.

(4) Melt the chocolate in the top of a double boiler.

(5) Dip the top of each cone in the melted chocolate to cover the filling and gently press in one hazelnut. Serve immediately or store for up to 24 hours at room temperature.

Peruvian Chocolate Alfajores

The famous Argentinean Alfajores cookie gets a new interpretation in my kitchen, one that chocolate lovers particularly enjoy. Use ready-made Dulce de Leche, found in gourmet supermarkets.

Makes 20

1 recipe Almond Shortcrust Pastry (Basics page 13), with added cocoa

1 recipe Marzipan (Basics page 30)

1/4 cup Dulce de Leche

5 ounces bittersweet chocolate, cut in small pieces

1/2 cup dried coconut

Baking sheet

Parchment paper

1/2-inch round cutter

Medium bowl

Shallow bowl

Double boiler

(1) Preheat the oven to 375°F. Line a baking sheet with parchment paper.

(2) Roll out the shortcrust pastry 1/8 inch thick on a lightly floured work surface.

(3) Use a 1/2-inch round cutter to cut out 40 circles. If necessary, gather up the remaining dough pieces, roll out, and cut additional circles. Place on the parchment-lined baking sheet.

(4) Bake for 15 minutes. Carefully transfer to a wire rack and let cool completely.

(5) In a medium bowl, combine the marzipan and the Dulce de Leche, and mix well with a wire whisk until smooth.

(6) Place a teaspoon of the mixture on one of the circles, and spread out evenly with the back of the spoon. Top with another circle. Repeat with the remaining circles for a total of 20 sandwich-style cookies.

(7) Grind the coconut in a food processor till fine and place in a shallow bowl.

(8) Melt the chocolate in the top of a double boiler. Pour into a shallow bowl.

(9) Roll the edges of each cookie in the melted chocolate, so that the filling is completely covered, then immediately roll in the coconut, to cover the chocolate.

(10) Chill the cookies for 30 minutes in the refrigerator and serve. The cookies may be kept at room temperature in an airtight jar for up to 2 days.

Coffee Ganache Cones

This delightful combination of coffee ganache and cake fills the kitchen with an irresistible aroma. Though the process is time-consuming, the results are well worth it.

Makes 12

1 recipe Cigarettes (Petits Fours page 87)

1 cup whipping cream

2 tablespoons Coffee Essence (Basics page 29)

1 tablespoon brandy

14 ounces bittersweet chocolate, cut in small pieces

Medium saucepan

Bowl

Pastry bag with a 1/3-inch round tip

Double boiler

(1) Prepare the cigarette dough and bake according to the recipe directions. Use oven mitts to shape each cigarette into an ice cream cone shape. Place seam side down on a work surface and let cool for 10 minutes.

(2) In a medium saucepan, prepare the ganache by bringing the whipping cream and coffee essence to a boil.

(3) Place the brandy and 9 ounces of the chocolate in a bowl, and pour over the boiling cream. Mix well, cool to room temperature, and place in the refrigerator for 1 hour.

(4) Transfer the cooled ganache to a pastry bag with a 1/3-inch round tip and fill each cone 3/4 full.

(5) Place the filled cones on a baking sheet that fits in your freezer. Place in the freezer for 20 minutes. At this point, the cones may be frozen for up to 1 week. If the cones have been frozen for more than 20 minutes, let them defrost for 30 minutes before proceeding to the next step.

(6) Melt the remaining 5 ounces of chocolate in the top of a double boiler.

(7) Dip the top of each cone in the melted chocolate to cover the filling. Serve immediately or store at room temperature for up to 24 hours.

Individual Chocolate Squares

This recipe produces more than 100 tiny chocolate treats, so it's perfect for entertaining.

Makes 120

1 recipe Ladyfinger Mixture [Basics page 18], with 1 tablespoon cocoa

1 cup whipping cream

9 ounces bittersweet chocolate, cut into pieces

1 tablespoon grated orange zest

2 tablespoons Grand Marnier or other orange liqueur

4 ounces white chocolate, for garnish

2 baking sheets

Parchment paper

9 x 13 x 1-inch baking pan

Small saucepan

Double boiler

(1) Preheat the oven to 375°F. Line 2 baking sheets with parchment paper. Grease a 9 x 13 x 1-inch baking pan. The baking sheets should be slightly larger than the baking pan.

(2) Prepare the ladyfinger mixture according to the recipe directions, adding 1 tablespoon of cocoa.

(3) Use a palette knife to thinly spread the mixture onto the baking sheets. The batter should be about 1/8 inch thick, or even a little less.

(4) Bake for 15 minutes. When baked, transfer the contents of both baking sheets, together with the pieces of parchment paper, to a wire rack. Cool for 30 minutes.

(5) In the meantime make the chocolate ganache. Place the whipping cream in a small saucepan and bring to a boil. Remove from heat and add the bittersweet chocolate. Mix well with a wire whisk until all of the chocolate is melted.

(6) Stir in the orange zest and Grand Marnier and mix well. Set aside.

(7) Turn the cakes over so that the parchment paper is facing up, then very slowly and carefully peel off the parchment paper. Carefully cut each sheet of cake so that it is exactly the dimensions of the greased baking pan.

(8) Carefully place one of the cake sheets into the pan, pressing it down to the bottom. Pour half of the chocolate ganache over the cake, using a palette knife to spread it evenly over the cake. Transfer the pan to the refrigerator for 30 minutes.

(9) Remove the pan from the refrigerator and carefully place the other sheet of cake on top of the chilled ganache. Press down lightly, then pour the remaining ganache over top. Use a palette knife to level the ganache, so that it is evenly spread. Return to the refrigerator for 2 hours.

(10) Remove from the refrigerator and place on a work surface. Using a sharp knife, divide the cake into 1-inch squares. You may want to use a ruler to mark the slices before you cut, so that each petit four is a perfect square. Carefully remove the squares from the pan and arrange on a serving dish.

(11) Separately, melt the white chocolate in the top of a double boiler over low heat. Use a teaspoon to place a drop of the melted chocolate on top of each square. Serve immediately or store for up to 2 days.

Cats' Tongues

Although these petits fours may look complicated they are actually quite easy to make. They go great alongside a fresh cup of espresso or hot cocoa with a touch of whipped cream.

Makes 20

4 egg whites

1/2 cup confectioner's sugar

1/2 cup melted butter

2/3 cup unbleached all-purpose flour

Large bowl

Baking sheet

Silicone baking sheet

Pastry bag with a 1/8-inch tip

(1) In a large bowl, combine the egg whites and confectioner's sugar, and whisk together till smooth.

(2) Gradually blend in the melted butter and then the flour. Cover with plastic wrap and chill in the refrigerator for 30 minutes.

(3) Preheat the oven to 375°F. Line a baking sheet with a silicone baking sheet.

(4) Transfer the chilled batter to a pastry bag with a 1/8-inch tip. Pipe twenty 6-inch strips, 1 inch apart. Bake for 10 minutes.

(5) Using a palette knife, remove one tuile at a time while still warm and wrap it around the handle of a wooden spoon, like a corkscrew. Leave on the spoon for 10 minutes, then carefully remove. Repeat with the remaining tuiles. If you have several wooden spoons, you can make several corkscrew tuiles at the same time. If the tuiles become brittle before you have a chance to wrap them, return them to the oven for a few seconds before wrapping around the spoon.

(6) Serve within 12 hours after baking.

Salame di Cioccolata

In Sicily, a simple version of this quick chocolate dessert is called a "chocolate salami." I've upgraded it to create an impressive and tasty petit four. It can be stored in the freezer for up to 2 weeks, and is great to have on hand when guests arrive.

Makes 48 slices

1/2 cup raisins

9 ounces bittersweet chocolate, cut in small pieces

3 tablespoons butter

1/3 cup sugar

1/3 cup blanched almonds

1 cup butter cookie crumbs

3 tablespoons chopped candied citrus rinds

2 egg yolks

Double boiler

Wax paper

(1) Soak the raisins in hot water for 10 minutes and drain.

(2) Melt the chocolate and butter in the top of a double boiler.

(3) Add the sugar, almonds, cookie crumbs, citrus rinds, and drained raisins and mix well. Remove from heat.

(4) Whisk in the egg yolks with a hand whisk. Let cool.

(5) Shape the mixture into a roll that is 12 inches by 1 inch. Cover completely with wax paper and let chill in the refrigerator for about 2 hours, or until firm.

(6) When ready to serve, remove the wax paper and slice into 1/4-inch slices. Arrange on a serving plate and serve.

Cookies

Confidentially, I'm just crazy about cookies. There are those that just beg to be served with a cup of tea, and others that invite a cup of coffee. There are the type of cookies I'd grab for breakfast, and others I'd rather have in the afternoon. A fragrant little Madeleine (page 000), fresh from the oven, is definitely my idea of a light and eminently satisfying way to end a meal. Fun to bake with children, cookies are also a thoughtful and delicious gift.

For this book, I've chosen a unique selection of our family's favorite cookies from the French and Italian traditions, especially those cookies that can serve as the basis for improvisation.

For best results, always use the best quality creamery butter. Make sure to store cookies in an airtight jar to preserve freshness and taste.

Amaretti

These wonderful cookies are a classic in Italy, where they are often served with a cup of piping hot espresso. This is also one of the easiest recipes in the book.

Makes 40

2 egg whites

1 cup sugar

1 1/2 cups ground blanched almonds

2 tablespoons unbleached all-purpose flour

1/4 cup Amaretto

1/4 cup natural almonds, with skins, for garnish

Cookie sheet

Parchment paper

Electric mixer

Pastry bag with a 1/4-inch open star tip

(1) Preheat oven to 375°F. Line a cookie sheet with parchment paper.

(2) Whip the egg whites in an electric mixer using the wire whisk, till soft peaks form.

(3) Add the sugar gradually and continue whipping until stiff.

(4) Gradually fold in the ground almonds with a rubber spatula.

(5) Gently fold in the flour and Amaretto till the mixture is smooth and uniform in texture.

(6) Transfer to a pastry bag with a 1/4-inch open star tip. Pipe 1-inch circles onto the cookie sheet, about 1/2 inch apart. Place an almond in the center of each.

(7) Bake for 15 minutes until deep brown with a reddish tinge. Place the cookies on a wire rack till cool. Serve immediately, or store in an airtight jar at room temperature for about 1 week.

Coffee Shortbread

These luscious butter cookies with a hint of coffee come from the French city of Nantes. They are great served with a cup of good coffee on a lazy afternoon.

Makes 15

1/2 cup butter

1/2 cup confectioner's sugar

2 egg yolks

2 tablespoons water

1 teaspoon pure vanilla extract

1/2 teaspoon salt

1 1/2 cups unbleached all-purpose flour

1/2 teaspoon baking powder

2 tablespoons Coffee Essence (Basics page 29)

Cookie sheet

Parchment paper

Food processor

4-inch round cutter

(1) Line a cookie sheet with parchment paper.

(2) Combine the butter and confectioner's sugar in the bowl of a food processor and process with the metal blade for 2 minutes until smooth.

(3) Add the egg yolks, water, vanilla extract, and salt, and process for an additional 2 minutes.

(4) Gradually add the flour and baking powder and process for another minute or two, until the dough forms a neat ball in the work bowl. Wrap the dough in plastic wrap and let rest in the refrigerator at least 30 minutes.

(5) Preheat oven to 375°F.

(6) Roll out the dough 1/8 inch thick on a lightly floured work surface.

(7) Use a 4-inch round cutter to cut out circles and place on the cookie sheet. On the top of each cookie, generously brush the coffee flavoring and use a fork to make a zigzag pattern.

(8) Bake for 15 minutes. Transfer to a wire rack and let cool. Stored in an airtight jar at room temperature, the cookies will stay fresh for at least 1 week.

Walnut Shortbread

If you're nuts about walnuts, you'll simply adore these crispy aromatic cookies. They can also be made with toasted pecans or peanuts.

Makes 30

3/4 cup butter

1/2 cup confectioner's sugar

1 egg

1 1/2 tablespoons water

2 tablespoons brandy

1 teaspoon salt

1 1/2 cups unbleached all-purpose flour

1 teaspoon baking powder

1/2 cup finely chopped walnuts

1 egg, beaten

1/2 cup brown sugar

1/2 cup ground walnuts

Cookie sheet

Parchment paper

Food processor

(1) Line a cookie sheet with parchment paper.

(2) Combine the butter and confectioner's sugar in the bowl of a food processor and process with the metal blade for 2 minutes until smooth.

(3) Add the egg, water, brandy, salt, half of the flour, and baking powder and process for an additional 2 minutes.

(4) Gradually add the remaining flour and finely chopped walnuts and process for another minute or two, until the dough forms a neat ball in the work bowl. Wrap the dough in plastic wrap and let rest in the refrigerator at least 30 minutes.

(5) Preheat the oven to 375°F.

(6) Roll out the dough on a floured work surface to form a 1 1/2-inch diameter log. Wrap in plastic wrap and chill for 15 minutes.

(7) Brush the log with the beaten egg. Mix together the brown sugar and ground walnuts and press the mixture on all sides of the log, to cover evenly.

(8) Using a sharp chef's knife, slice the log into 1/4-inch-thick cookies. Place 1/2 inch apart on the cookie sheet. Brush the tops with the remaining beaten egg and sprinkle with the remaining brown sugar-walnut mixture.

(9) Bake for 15 minutes. Transfer to a wire rack and let cool. Stored in an airtight jar, the cookies will stay fresh at room temperature for at least 1 week.

Tozzetti

There are many versions of tozzetti in Italy, where they are enjoyed along with café au lait or espresso. My personal version adds raisins to enrich the taste and add a little moisture to the basically dry texture of the original recipe. Although the process may sound complicated, they are actually easy to make, and stay fresh for a long time.

Makes 50

3 eggs

3/4 cup sugar

2 cups unbleached all-purpose flour

Pinch of salt

1 teaspoon baking powder

1/3 cup whole almonds

1/3 cup hazelnuts

1/4 cup small dark raisins

Cookie sheet

Parchment paper

Electric mixer

(1) Line a cookie sheet with parchment paper.

(2) Combine the eggs, sugar, flour, salt, and baking powder in the bowl of an electric mixer, and use the dough hook to mix the ingredients together for 3 minutes on low speed.

(3) Add the almonds, hazelnuts, and raisins, and mix on medium speed for an additional 3 minutes.

(4) Turn the dough out on a lightly floured surface and roll into a ball, then shape into a 10-inch-long loaf. Carefully place the loaf on the cookie sheet and let rest in the refrigerator for 30 minutes.

(5) Preheat the oven to 375°F. Remove the pan from the refrigerator and place it directly into the oven. Bake for 30 minutes.

(6) Cool the loaf on a wire rack for 30 minutes, then place in the freezer for 30 minutes.

(7) Remove from the freezer and place on a cutting board. Use a chef's knife to cut into 1/4-inch-thick slices.

(8) Place the slices on the same pan and return to the oven, still set at 375°F, for an additional 15 minutes. Cool on a wire rack. May be stored in an airtight jar for up to 2 weeks.

Dry Fruit Croquets

The addition of dried fruit makes this recipe a totally different cookie experience.

Makes 30

3/4 cup butter

1/2 cup confectioner's sugar

2 eggs

1 tablespoon water

1 teaspoon pure vanilla extract

2 tablespoons brandy

1 teaspoon salt

1 1/2 cups unbleached all-purpose flour

1 teaspoon baking powder

1/4 cup ground walnuts

1/4 cup coarsely chopped dried apricots

1/4 cup dark raisins

1 egg, beaten

1/4 cup sugar, for garnish

Cookie sheet

Parchment paper

Food processor

(1) Line a cookie sheet with parchment paper.

(2) Combine the butter and confectioner's sugar in the bowl of a food processor and process with the metal blade for 2 minutes until smooth.

(3) Add the eggs, water, vanilla extract, brandy, salt, half the flour, and baking powder and process for an additional 2 minutes.

(4) Add the remaining flour and process another minute.

(5) Add the walnuts, apricots, and raisins and continue to process until the dough forms a neat ball in the work bowl. Wrap the dough in plastic wrap and let rest in the refrigerator at least 30 minutes.

(6) Preheat the oven to 375°F.

(7) Roll out the dough on a floured work surface to form a 1 1/2-inch-diameter log. Wrap in plastic wrap and chill 15 minutes.

(8) Using a sharp chef's knife, slice the log into 1/4-inch-thick cookies. Place the cookies 1/2 inch apart on the cookie sheet. Brush the tops with the beaten egg, and sprinkle the remaining sugar.

(9) Bake for 15 minutes. Transfer to a wire rack and let cool. Stored in an airtight jar, the cookies will stay fresh at room temperature for at least 1 week.

Sablés

Simple but wonderful, these are the kind of cookies you'll always love to have in your cookie jar.

Makes 30

1/2 cup butter

1/2 cup confectioner's sugar

2 egg yolks

2 tablespoons water

1 teaspoon pure vanilla extract

2 tablespoons brandy

1/2 teaspoon salt

1 1/2 cups unbleached all-purpose flour

1/2 teaspoon baking powder

1 egg, beaten

1/4 cup sugar, for garnish

Cookie sheet

Parchment paper

Food processor

(1) Line a cookie sheet with parchment paper.

(2) Combine the butter and confectioner's sugar in the bowl of a food processor and process with the metal blade for 2 minutes until smooth.

(3) Add the egg yolks, water, vanilla extract, brandy, and salt, and process for an additional 2 minutes.

(4) Gradually add the flour and baking powder and process for another minute or two, until the dough forms a neat ball in the work bowl. Wrap the dough in plastic wrap and let rest in the refrigerator at least 30 minutes.

(5) Preheat the oven to 375°F.

(6) Roll out the dough on a floured work surface to form a 1 1/2-inch-diameter log. Wrap in plastic wrap and chill 15 minutes.

(7) Brush the log with the beaten egg and press the sugar evenly onto all sides of the log.

(8) Using a sharp chef's knife, slice the log into 1/4-inch-thick cookies. Place the cookies 1/2 inch apart on the cookie sheet. Brush the tops with the remaining beaten egg, and sprinkle with the remaining sugar.

(9) Bake for 15 minutes. Transfer to a wire rack and let cool. Stored in an airtight jar, the cookies will stay fresh at room temperature for at least 1 week.

Pigs' Ears

These cute cookies are one of the first recipes I learned to make in elementary school. They hold a place of honor on my personal memory lane.

Makes 25

1/2 recipe Puff Pastry
(Basics page 15)

1 egg, beaten

1/2 cup sugar

Cookie sheet

Parchment paper

(1) Preheat the oven to 400°F. Line a cookie sheet with parchment paper.

(2) Roll the puff pastry into a 16 x 10-inch rectangle on a lightly floured surface.

(3) Brush with the beaten egg and sprinkle sugar evenly over the top.

(4) Place your fingers on one of the longer sides of the rectangle and roll it up like a jellyroll, stopping when you reach the center. Move to the other longer side and roll it up as well, stopping in the center. Now the dough should be rolled into two scrolls that face each other.

(5) Press the scrolls together and roll one on top of the other to form a log shape.

(6) Use a sharp chef's knife to cut 1/4-inch-thick slices, and place on the cookie sheet.

(7) Bake for 15 minutes. Carefully remove and cool on a wire rack. Store in an airtight jar for about 1 week.

Note: For best results, make sure the dough is covered in a generous layer of sugar before baking, and bake until the cookies are golden brown.

Madeleines

Scallop-shaped Madeleines, baked in their own special pan, were our favorite cookies when I studied in Paris, and my wife and I must have sampled hundreds in our quest for the best Madeleine in town. Serve Madeleines to your guests at the end of the evening and they're sure to leave with a smile.

Makes 30

2 tablespoons butter

4 eggs

3/4 cup sugar

1/2 teaspoon salt

1 tablespoon honey

1 teaspoon pure vanilla extract

1 1/3 cups unbleached all-purpose flour

1 teaspoon baking powder

1 cup melted butter

Madeleine pan

Electric mixer

Pastry bag with a 1/4-inch round tip

(1) Grease a madeleine pan with the 2 tablespoons of butter and set aside.

(2) Combine the eggs and sugar in the bowl of an electric mixer and whip using a balloon whip till smooth.

(3) Whip in the salt, honey, and vanilla extract.

(4) Gradually fold in the flour and baking powder by hand with a rubber spatula.

(5) Fold in the melted butter and mix gently until the batter is smooth.

(6) Cover the bowl with plastic wrap and place in the refrigerator to rest for 30 minutes.

(7) Preheat the oven to 400°F. Transfer the mixture into a pastry bag with a 1/4-inch round tip, and fill the greased madeleine molds 3/4 full. Madeleines need room to rise, so be careful not to overfill the molds.

(8) Bake for 10 minutes or until golden brown.

(9) Madeleines are best consumed soon after baking. They can be stored in an airtight container in the refrigerator for up to 2 days.

Note: Mini-madeleine pans are also available.

Quiches

A book on patisserie could never be complete without including some savory selections. First and foremost, this includes the quiche. In this chapter, you'll find some of my favorite quiches—those served time and time again to friends and family with rave reviews.

Baked in 4-inch individual pans, quiche makes a fine starter. Made in the traditional 10-inch pan, a slice of quiche served with a salad of mixed greens makes an ideal light meal. Feel free to improvise, using the Savory Shortcrust Pastry (Basics page 12), which can be made in advance and frozen, freshly-made Quiche Filling (Basics page 25), and your own creative combination of ingredients.

Goat Cheese Quiche

This blend of aromatic goat cheese and golden pastry crust makes one of the most popular and beloved quiches in France. For best flavor, blend two different kinds of aged (ripened) goat cheeses, like St. Maure and Boucheron. You can also use unripened chevre, although the quiche will be less aromatic. Of course, this quiche may also be made with piquant milk cheeses.

Serves 6

1 recipe Savory Shortcrust Pastry (Basics page 14)

1 egg, beaten

8 ounces aged goat cheese, cut into 1/4-inch slices

24 cherry tomatoes, halved

1 tablespoon chopped fresh thyme leaves

2 tablespoons chopped fresh parsley

4 garlic cloves, crushed

1 recipe Basic Quiche Filling (Basics page 25)

Six 4-inch quiche pans

Parchment paper

Beans or commercial pie weights

(1) Roll out the shortcrust pastry 1/8 inch thick on a lightly floured work surface.

(2) Divide the dough evenly among six 4-inch quiche pans, using your fingers to press the dough into place. Cut off any excess dough around the edges.

(3) Place the pans in the refrigerator for 15 minutes. Preheat the oven to 375°F.

(4) Cut out pieces of parchment paper to fit the bottoms of the pans. Place the paper over the chilled dough and weigh down with beans or commercial pie weights. Bake for 20 minutes.

(5) Remove the weights and paper, and brush the bottoms and sides with the egg. Bake for an additional 3 minutes.

(6) Transfer the pans to a work surface. Arrange the cheese, tomatoes, herbs, and garlic in the bottoms of the pans, and pour the prepared filling on top. Bake for 20 minutes. Serve immediately or let cool to room temperature and reheat before serving. Best consumed same day (see photo of bottom quiche on page 123).

Mascarpone and Smoked Salmon Quiche

By combining two traditional brunch favorites, this quiche is perfect for serving at a mid-morning weekend meal.

Serves 6

1 recipe Savory Shortcrust Pastry (Basics page 14)

1 egg, beaten

7 ounces smoked salmon, sliced

1/2 cup Mascarpone cheese

1 recipe Basic Quiche Filling (Basics page 25)

10-inch quiche pan

Parchment paper

Beans or commercial pie weights

(1) Roll out the shortcrust pastry 1/8 inch thick on a lightly floured work surface.

(2) Carefully transfer the dough to a 10-inch quiche pan and use your fingers to press into place. Cut off any excess dough around the edges.

(3) Place the pan in the refrigerator for 15 minutes. In the meantime, preheat the oven to 375°F.

(4) Cut out a piece of parchment paper to fit the bottom of the pan. Place the paper over the chilled dough, and weigh down with beans or commercial pie weights. Bake for 20 minutes.

(5) Remove the weights and paper, and brush the bottom and sides with the egg. Bake for an additional 3 minutes.

(6) Transfer the pan to a work surface. Arrange the slices of smoked salmon on the bottom. Spoon the cheese evenly over the salmon, and pour the prepared filling over top. Return the pan to the oven and bake for 20 minutes. Serve immediately or let cool to room temperature and reheat before serving. Best consumed on the same day.

Quiche Provençale

This is my variation of the classic, inspired by a memorable quiche I enjoyed in a small village in southern France.

Serves 10 (as a starter) or 6 (as a main dish)

1 recipe Savory Shortcrust Pastry (Basics page 14)

1 egg, beaten

1/2 cup pitted black olives in wine

1/2 cup thinly sliced sun-dried tomatoes

4 garlic cloves, crushed

1/2 cup aged goat cheese, cut into cubes

1 tablespoon chopped fresh thyme leaves

8 olive oil-packed anchovy fillets

20 fresh basil leaves, chopped

1 recipe Basic Quiche Filling (Basics page 25)

10-inch quiche pan

Parchment paper

Beans or commercial pie weights

(1) Roll out the shortcrust pastry 1/8 inch thick on a lightly floured work surface.

(2) Carefully transfer the dough to a 10-inch quiche pan and use your fingers to press the dough into place. Cut off any excess dough around the edges.

(3) Place the pan in the refrigerator for 15 minutes. In the meantime, preheat the oven to 375°F.

(4) Cut out a piece of parchment paper to fit the bottom of the pan. Place the paper over the chilled dough and weigh down with beans or commercial pie weights. Bake for 20 minutes.

(5) Remove the weights and paper, and brush the bottom and sides with the egg. Bake for an additional 3 minutes.

(6) Transfer the pan to a work surface. Sprinkle the olives, sun-dried tomatoes, garlic, goat cheese, thyme, anchovy fillets, and basil evenly over the baked crust. Pour the prepared filling on top. Return the pan to the oven and bake for 20 minutes. Serve immediately or let cool to room temperature and reheat before serving. Best consumed same day.

Wild Mushroom Quiche

Although once we had to forage for them, today you can find exotic wild mushrooms in every upscale grocery store. Whatever combination of mushrooms you'll be using, just remember to lightly sauté them first in olive oil or butter and drain to enhance their flavor.

Serves 6

1 recipe Savory Shortcrust Pastry (Basics page 14)

1 egg, beaten

1/2 cup butter

4 garlic cloves, minced

3 cups assorted wild mushrooms

1 teaspoon salt

1 teaspoon white pepper

2 tablespoons finely chopped parsley

1/4 cup freshly grated Parmesan cheese

1 recipe Basic Quiche Filling (Basics page 25)

Six 4-inch quiche pans

Parchment paper

Beans or commercial pie weights

Heavy frying pan

(1) Roll out the shortcrust pastry 1/8 inch thick on a lightly floured work surface.

(2) Divide the dough evenly among six 4-inch quiche pans, using your fingers to press the dough into place. Cut off any excess dough around the edges.

(3) Place the pans in the refrigerator for 15 minutes. In the meantime, preheat the oven to 375°F.

(4) Cut out pieces of parchment paper to fit the bottom of the pans. Place the paper over the chilled dough and weigh down with beans or commercial pie weights. Bake for 20 minutes.

(5) Remove the weights and paper, and brush the bottoms and sides with the egg. Bake for an additional 3 minutes. Transfer the pans to a work surface.

(6) Heat a heavy frying pan over medium heat and add a teaspoon or two of the butter. Add the garlic and sauté for 1 minute till softened.

(7) Add the mushrooms, salt, and pepper and sauté for 10 minutes, stirring often, until the mushrooms are softened and aromatic. Add the remaining butter and cook for an additional 3 minutes. Now add the parsley and stir.

(8) Drain the mushrooms and divide equally among the pans. Sprinkle the cheese and pour the prepared filling on top. Return the pans to the oven and bake for 20 minutes. Serve immediately or let cool to room temperature and reheat before serving. Best consumed hours after baking (see top quiche on opposite page).

Asparagus & Blue Cheese Quiche

Pairing asparagus and blue cheese is not only delicious; it also adds a regal air to any occasion. Served with a bottle of quality Chardonnay, it also makes a great menu item for a romantic picnic.

Serves 10 (as a starter) or 6 (as a main dish)

1 recipe Savory Shortcrust Pastry (Basics page 14)

1 egg, beaten

1/2 pound fresh green medium-width asparagus, trimmed

1/2 cup crumbled Roquefort, or other Blue Cheese

1 recipe Basic Quiche Filling (see Basics page 25)

10-inch quiche pan

Parchment paper

Beans or commercial pie weights

(1) Roll out the shortcrust pastry 1/8 inch thick on a lightly floured work surface.

(2) Carefully transfer the dough to a 10-inch quiche pan and use your fingers to press into place. Cut off any excess dough around the edges.

(3) Place the pan in the refrigerator for 15 minutes. In the meantime, preheat the oven to 375°F.

(4) Cut out a piece of parchment paper to fit the bottom of the pan. Place the paper over the chilled dough, and weigh down with beans or commercial pie weights. Bake for 20 minutes.

(5) Remove the weights and paper, and brush the bottom and sides with the egg. Bake for an additional 3 minutes.

(6) Transfer the pan to a work surface. Arrange the asparagus on the bottom and sprinkle the cheese evenly over the asparagus. Pour the prepared filling on top. Return the pan to the oven and bake for 20 minutes. Serve immediately or let cool to room temperature and reheat before serving. Best consumed hours after baking.

Eggplant & Emmenthal Quiche

This quiche is my own invention, created for a friend who is a true eggplant fan. The important point here is to roast the eggplant slices really well before placing them on the pastry crust.

Serves 6

1 recipe Savory Shortcrust Pastry (Basics page 14)

1 egg, beaten

1 large eggplant, cut widthwise into twelve 1/2-inch slices

2 tablespoons extra-virgin olive oil

3/4 cup coarsely grated Emmenthal cheese

1 recipe Basic Quiche Filling (Basics page 25)

Six 4-inch quiche pans

Parchment paper

Beans or commercial pie weights

Ridged grill pan

(1) Roll out the shortcrust pastry 1/8 inch thick on a lightly floured work surface.

(2) Carefully divide the dough among six 4-inch quiche pans, using your fingers to press the dough into place. Cut off any excess dough around the edges.

(3) Place the pans in the refrigerator for 15 minutes. In the meantime, preheat the oven to 375°F.

(4) Cut out pieces of parchment paper to fit the bottoms of the pans. Place the paper over the chilled dough and weigh down with beans or commercial pie weights. Bake for 20 minutes.

(5) Remove the weights and paper, and brush the bottoms and sides with the egg. Bake for an additional 3 minutes. Transfer the pans to a work surface.

(6) Heat a ridged grill pan on medium flame until hot. Roast the eggplant slices until golden and tender. Transfer to a plate and pour the olive oil over the top. Let stand for a few minutes.

(7) Arrange two eggplant slices, one atop of the other, in the bottom of each pan. Sprinkle with the cheese, and pour the prepared filling on top. Bake for 20 minutes. Serve immediately or let cool to room temperature and reheat before serving. Best consumed same day.

Seafood Quiche

This quiche comes to us from the Normandy coast, a region of France that boasts fine seafood—and plenty of it.

Serves 6

1 recipe Savory Shortcrust Pastry (Basics page 14)

1 egg, beaten

1 pound mixed seafood, fresh or frozen, thawed, and drained

1/2 cup grated Parmesan cheese

1 recipe Basic Quiche Filling (Basics page 25)

6 4-inch quiche pans

Parchment paper

Beans or commercial pie weights

(1) Roll out the shortcrust pastry 1/8 inch thick on a lightly floured work surface.

(2) Divide the dough evenly among 6 4-inch quiche pans, using your fingers to press the dough into place. Cut off any excess dough around the edges.

(3) Place the pans in the refrigerator for 15 minutes. In the meantime, preheat the oven to 375°F.

(4) Cut out pieces of parchment paper to fit the bottoms of the pans. Place the paper over the chilled dough, and weigh down with beans or commercial pie weights. Bake for 20 minutes.

(5) Remove the weights and paper, and brush the bottoms and sides with the egg. Bake for an additional 3 minutes.

(6) Transfer the pans to a work surface and arrange seafood in the bottoms. Sprinkle with the cheese, and pour the prepared filling on top. Bake for 20 minutes. Serve immediately or let cool to room temperature and reheat before serving. Best consumed same day.

Olive & Feta Cheese Quiche

As compensation for the icy cold winters of Paris, we often escaped to the sun and sea of the Greek islands when school was out. That was the inspiration behind this quiche, which blends the marvelous flavors of Greek feta cheese, olives, and oregano, with French technique.

Serves 6

1 recipe Savory Shortcrust Pastry (Basics page 14)

1 egg, beaten

1/2 cup pitted whole Kalamata olives

3/4 cup Greek feta cheese, crumbled by hand

2 tablespoons chopped fresh oregano, or 2 teaspoons dried Greek oregano

1 recipe Basic Quiche Filling (Basics page 25)

Six 4-inch quiche pans

Parchment paper

Beans or commercial pie weights

(1) Roll out the shortcrust pastry 1/8 inch thick on a lightly floured work surface.

(2) Divide the dough evenly among six 4-inch quiche pans, using your fingers to press the dough into place. Cut off any excess dough around the edges.

(3) Place the pans in the refrigerator for 15 minutes. In the meantime, preheat the oven to 375°F.

(4) Cut out pieces of parchment paper to fit the bottoms of the pans. Place the paper over the chilled dough and weigh down with beans or commercial pie weights. Bake for 20 minutes.

(5) Remove the weights and paper, and brush the bottoms and sides with the egg. Bake for an additional 3 minutes.

(6) Transfer the pans to a work surface. Divide the olives evenly among the pans, and top with the cheese and oregano. Pour the prepared filling on top and bake for 20 minutes. Serve immediately or let cool to room temperature and reheat before serving. Best consumed same day.

Quiche Lorraine

One of the most all-time popular quiches, this quiche hails from the Alsace region of France, on the French-German border. Warm and satisfying, it is traditionally served in the winter.

Serves 10 (as a starter) or 6 (as a main dish)

1 recipe Savory Shortcrust Pastry (Basics page 14)

1 egg, beaten

1/2 cup slab bacon, cut into small cubes

1/2 cup grated Emmenthal or Gouda cheese (or other aromatic cheese)

1 recipe Basic Quiche Filling (see Basics page 25)

10-inch quiche pan

Parchment paper

Beans or commercial pie weights

(1) Roll out the shortcrust pastry 1/8 inch thick on a lightly floured work surface.

(2) Carefully transfer the dough to a 10-inch quiche pan, using your fingers to press the dough into place. Cut off any excess dough around the edges.

(3) Place the pan in the refrigerator for 15 minutes. In the meantime, preheat the oven to 375°F.

(4) Cut out a piece of parchment paper to fit the bottom of the pan. Place the paper over the chilled dough, and weigh down with beans or commercial pie weights. Bake for 20 minutes.

(5) Remove the weights and paper, and brush the bottom and sides with the egg. Bake for an additional 3 minutes.

(6) Transfer the pan to a work surface and scatter the bacon in the bottom. Sprinkle the cheese over the bacon, and pour the quiche filling on top. Return to the oven and bake for 20 minutes. Serve immediately or let cool to room temperature and reheat before serving. Best consumed same day.

Traditional Cakes

In this chapter you'll find recipes for some of the finest traditional cakes found in France and Italy. Each one is unique. Mille-Feuilles is a dream for lovers of vanilla cream. Pithiviers is a traditional holiday cake in the south of France. The classic Baba au Rhum makes an elegant dessert for a festive meal. The regal Meringato Fiorentino is like the cherry on top; served with a dessert wine like Vincento, it's the perfect end to a meal fit for kings.

Vanilla Mille-Feuilles

The Mille-Feuilles, whose name means 1,000 leaves, is a classic throughout Europe. Also known as the Napoleon, it is especially popular in Austria, Germany, Switzerland, France, and England.

Serves 12

1/2 recipe Puff Pastry
(Basics page 15)

1 cup whipping cream

2 cups Crème Patissière
(Basics page 23)

1/4 cup confectioner's sugar

Baking sheet

Parchment paper

Electric mixer

Serving platter that fits in
your freezer

(1) Preheat the oven to 400°F. Line a baking sheet with parchment paper.

(2) Roll out the puff pastry 1/8 inch thick on a lightly floured work surface and place on the lined baking sheet. Use a fork to pierce holes along the entire bottom of the dough.

(3) Bake for 18 minutes. Remove from the oven and flip the dough over using 2 spatulas. With the other side facing up, bake for another 10 minutes. The baked dough will now be very crispy. Transfer to a wire rack to cool, then place on a cutting board.

(4) In the bowl of an electric mixer, whisk the whipping cream and pastry cream together till smooth.

(5) Use a chef's knife to cut the baked dough into 3 long strips, of equal width.

(6) Place one strip of dough on a serving platter that can fit into your freezer. Spread a 1-inch-thick layer of cream filling on top of the dough. Place in the freezer for 20 minutes.

(7) Top with another strip of dough and another 1-inch layer of cream filling and return to the freezer for an additional 20 minutes.

(8) Remove from the freezer and top with the remaining strip of dough.

(9) Run a palette knife along the sides of the cake so that the cream is neatly aligned along the sides, with no bumps, lumps, or holes. Return to the freezer uncovered for 2 hours, until completely frozen. At this stage, the cake may be frozen for up to 2 weeks in an odor-free container.

(10) When ready to serve, remove the cake from the freezer and place on a cutting board. Use a serrated knife to cut through the top layer of pastry. Switch to a chef's knife and use both hands to press the knife down to the bottom. The slices should be about 1 inch thick. Sprinkle confectioner's sugar on top and serve immediately.

Chocolate Mille-Feuilles

An unusual variation on the classic theme.

Serves 12

1/2 recipe Puff Pastry
(Basics page 15)

1 cup Chocolate Ganache
(Basics page 22)

2 cups Crème Patissière
(Basics page 23)

1/4 cup confectioner's sugar

Baking sheet

Parchment paper

Medium bowl

Serving platter that fits in
your freezer

(1) Preheat the oven to 400°F. Line a baking sheet with parchment paper.

(2) Roll the puff pastry dough 1/8 inch thick on a lightly floured surface and place on the lined baking sheet. Use a fork to pierce holes along the entire bottom of the dough.

(3) Bake for 18 minutes. Using 2 spatulas, carefully flip the dough over and bake the other side for 10 minutes. The baked dough will be very crispy. Transfer the dough to a wire rack to cool, then place on a cutting board.

(4) In a medium bowl, whisk the chocolate ganache and the pastry cream together until smooth.

(5) Use a chef's knife to cut the baked dough into 3 long strips, of equal width.

(6) Place one strip of dough on a serving platter that can fit into your freezer. Spread a 1-inch-thick layer of cream filling on top of the dough. Place in the freezer for 20 minutes.

(7) Top with another strip of dough and layer of filling. Return to the freezer for an additional 20 minutes. Remove from the freezer and top with the remaining strip of dough.

(8) Run a palette knife along the sides of the cake so that the cream is neatly aligned along the sides, with no bumps, lumps, or holes. Return to the freezer uncovered for 2 hours, until completely frozen. At this stage, the cake may be frozen for up to 2 weeks in an odor-free container.

(9) When ready to serve, remove the cake from the freezer and place on a cutting board. Use a serrated knife to cut through the top layer of pastry. Switch to a chef's knife and use both hands to press the knife down to the bottom. The slices should be about 1-inch thick. Sprinkle confectioner's sugar on top and serve immediately.

French Cherry Cake

When cherries are in season, this is the cake to make. Topped with a scoop of French Vanilla ice cream, it's a perfect summer dessert.

Serves 10

4 eggs

1 1/4 cups sugar

1 cup butter, room temperature

1/4 cup whipping cream

2 1/4 cups unbleached all-purpose flour

1 teaspoon baking powder

2 tablespoons cherry liqueur

1 pound fresh ripe cherries, pitted

10-inch springform baking pan

Electric mixer

(1) Preheat the oven to 375°F. Grease a 10-inch springform baking pan.

(2) In the bowl of an electric mixer, using the wire whisk attachment, beat the eggs and sugar on high speed until soft and foamy.

(3) Reduce the speed to medium and, with the machine running, add the butter and whipping cream. Beat until the mixture is smooth.

(4) Reduce to low speed and gradually add the flour and baking powder. Continue to beat until the mixture is smooth.

(5) Add the liqueur and beat until smooth.

(6) Pour half of the batter into the pan. Spread half of the cherries evenly over top, then pour over the rest of the batter. Place the remaining cherries over the batter, spreading them out so that they are evenly distributed.

(7) Bake for 30 minutes, or until a toothpick inserted in the center comes out clean. Serve immediately, or cool and reheat before serving. Best served on the same day.

Pithiviers

A native of southern France, Pithiviers only looks complicated. It is actually easy to make, and quite delicious. No wonder it's a holiday favorite in France.

Serves 10

1/2 recipe Puff Pastry
(Basics page 15)

1 recipe Almond Crème
(Basics page 26)

2 tablespoons Amaretto

1 egg, beaten

Baking sheet

Parchment paper

Pastry bag with a 1/3-inch round tip

(1) Preheat the oven to 400°F. Line a baking sheet with parchment paper.

(2) Roll the puff pastry dough 1/8 inch thick on a lightly floured surface.

(3) Cut a 10-inch-diameter circle out of parchment paper, and use it as template to cut 2 circles out of the dough with a sharp knife.

(4) Place one of the circles on the prepared baking sheet.

(5) Blend the almond crème and Amaretto and place in a pastry bag with a 1/3-inch round tip. Pipe the filling onto the circle, working in a spiral from the inside out, leaving 1 inch along the outside edge unfilled.

(6) Brush the edge of the circle with the egg, and place the second circle on top. Use a sharp knife to cut out 1-inch triangles from the edges, in a repeated zigzag pattern.

(7) Brush the top of the cake twice with the remaining egg, and use a sharp knife to make slashes from the center outward, like the rays of the sun.

(8) Bake for 30 minutes. Remove from the oven and let cool on a wire rack.

(9) Place on a cake plate and serve immediately. Store covered and at room temperature for serving the same day.

Coffee Dacquoise

Dacquoise is a family of mousse cakes that makes up a large part of the display window in every French pastry shop. While both ladyfinger and génoise are also used to make mousse cakes, they are based on whole eggs and flour. Dacquoise uses egg whites and ground almonds, giving it a unique taste and texture.

Makes 8

1 recipe Dacquoise Mixture (Basics page 19)

1/2 cup confectioner's sugar

1 cup whipping cream

2 tablespoons Coffee Essence (Basics page 29)

1 tablespoon good quality coffee liqueur

1/2 cup chocolate syrup, for garnish

4 baking sheets (see specifications in Step 1)

Parchment paper

Pastry bag with a 1/3-inch round tip

Electric mixer

Eight 3-inch baking rings

Cellophane cake collars

3-inch round cutter

(1) Preheat the oven to 375°F. Line 4 baking sheets with parchment paper. One baking sheet must measure at least 10 x 15 inches. Two baking sheets must have a combined area of 210 square inches, so sheets that measure 9 x 13 inches or 10 x 15 inches are fine. The fourth baking sheet must be able to fit into your freezer.

(2) Prepare the dacquoise mixture according to the recipe directions and transfer to a pastry bag with a 1/3-inch round tip.

(3) Pipe the mixture onto the 10 x 15-inch baking sheet in side-by-side horizontal strips. The strips should cover the whole baking sheet, and there should be no space between each strip. In the same manner, pipe two large rectangles onto the other two baking sheets.

(4) Sprinkle the confectioner's sugar passed through a strainer over the batter and bake for 15 minutes, or until golden brown. Transfer the cakes, with the parchment paper, to a wire rack and cool for 30 minutes.

(5) To make the coffee mousse, place the whipping cream in the bowl of an electric mixer and, using the whisk attachment, whip until almost stiff. Using a hand whisk, blend in the coffee essence and coffee liqueur until smooth.

(6) Line eight 3-inch baking rings with cellophane cake collars and place on the baking sheet that fits into your freezer.

(7) Using a sharp chef's knife, trim the 10 x 15-inch cake so that it measures 12 x 9 1/2 inches. Now cut the cake into eight 1 1/2 x 9 1/2-inch strips. Using a 3-inch round cutter, cut out 16 discs from the other rectangular cakes.

(8) Hold one of the cake strips in your hands and gently bend it into a cylinder, with the side that touched the parchment paper touching

your hands. Gently press each cylinder of cake into one of the baking rings. Repeat to line the other rings.

(9) Gently press a cake disc into the bottom of each ring with the side that touched the parchment paper facing up. Fill the rings halfway with mousse and place in the freezer for 20 minutes.

(10) Remove the cakes from the freezer and place another cake disc onto each one. Fill to the top with mousse and level with a palette knife. Place in the freezer until completely frozen. At this stage, the cakes may be frozen for up to 2 weeks.

(11) Remove the cakes from the freezer 30 minutes before serving and remove the rings and cake collars. Draw a crisscross pattern with the chocolate syrup on top of each cake and serve. May be stored for up to 3 days in the refrigerator.

Hazelnut Dacquoise

This fabulous cake is a festival of flavors. I've given it a modest garnish, but you can add a ganache, or sprinkle the top with chopped nuts.

Makes 8

1 recipe Dacquoise Mixture (Basics page 19)

1/2 cup confectioner's sugar

1 cup whipping cream

1/4 cup Nutella or other nut spread

1 tablespoon Amaretto

1/2 cup chocolate syrup, for garnish

3 baking sheets (see specifications in Step 1)

Parchment paper

Pastry bag with a 1/3-inch round tip

Electric mixer

Eight 3-inch baking rings

Cellophane cake collars

3-inch round cutter

(1) Preheat the oven to 375°F. Line 3 baking sheets with parchment paper. Two of the sheets must have a combined area of 210 inches, so sheets that measure 9 x 13 inches or 10 x 15 inches are fine. The third must be able to fit into your freezer.

(2) Prepare the dacquoise mixture according to the recipe directions and transfer to a pastry bag with a 1/3-inch round tip.

(3) Pipe the mixture onto the baking sheets in side-by-side horizontal strips, leaving no spaces between each strip, to make two large rectangles.

(4) Sprinkle the confectioner's sugar passed through a strainer over the batter and bake for 15 minutes, or until golden brown. Transfer the cakes, with the parchment paper, to a wire rack and cool for 30 minutes.

(5) To make the hazelnut mousse, place the whipping cream in the bowl of an electric mixer and, using the whisk attachment, whip until almost stiff. Using a hand whisk, blend in the Nutella and Amaretto until smooth.

(6) Line eight 3-inch baking rings with cellophane cake collars and place on the baking sheet that fits into your freezer.

(7) Using a 3-inch round cutter, cut out 16 discs from the cakes. Gently press one cake disc into the bottom of each baking ring, with the side that touched the parchment paper facing up. Fill each ring halfway with mousse and place in the freezer for 20 minutes.

(8) Remove the cakes from the freezer and place another cake disc onto each one. Fill to the top with mousse and level with a palette knife. Place in the freezer until completely frozen. At this stage, the cakes may be frozen for up to 2 weeks.

(9) Remove the cakes from the freezer 30 minutes before serving and remove the rings and cake collars. Drizzle the chocolate syrup on top of each cake and serve. May be stored for up to 3 days in the refrigerator.

Meringato Fiorentino

This classic hails from Florence, Italy. It features whipped cream and grated chocolate, artfully placed between layers of meringue. Simply magnifico!

Serves 8

1 recipe Italian Meringue Mixture (Basics page 20)

1/2 cup confectioner's sugar

3 tablespoons cocoa

2 cups whipping cream

2 tablespoons sugar

6 ounces bittersweet chocolate, coarsely grated

1 tablespoon grappa

Parchment paper

2 baking sheets, one of which fits into your freezer

2 bowls

Pastry bag with a 1/3-inch round tip

Electric mixer

10-inch baking ring

Cellophane cake collar

Pastry bag with a 1/4-inch open star tip

(1) Preheat the oven to 275°F. Draw two 10-inch circles on the underside of a piece of parchment paper and use it to line a baking sheet. These circles will guide you in Steps 3 and 4. Line a baking sheet that fits into your freezer with parchment paper and set aside.

(2) Prepare the meringue mixture according to the recipe directions and divide equally into 2 bowls. Fold the cocoa into one of the bowls using a rubber spatula.

(3) Transfer the plain meringue to a pastry bag with a 1/3-inch round tip. Working from the outside in, pipe a 10-inch filled disc on the baking sheets. Use the remaining batter to pipe meringue kisses along the edge of the sheet.

(4) Repeat Step 3 with the chocolate meringue, then sprinkle confectioner's sugar passed through a strainer over the batter and bake for 2 hours. Transfer the meringue, with the parchment paper, to a wire rack and cool for 30 minutes.

(5) To make the mousse, place the whipping cream and the sugar in the bowl of an electric mixer and, using the whisk attachment, whip until stiff. Using a rubber spatula, fold in 4 1/2 ounces of the chocolate and the grappa until smooth. Place in the refrigerator until ready to use.

(6) Line a 10-inch baking ring with a cellophane cake collar and place on the baking sheet that fits into your freezer.

(7) Gently press the chocolate meringue disc into the bottom of the baking ring. Pour in a 1/2-inch layer of mousse and level using a rubber spatula. Place in the freezer for 20 minutes.

(8) Remove the cake from the freezer and place the plain meringue disc over top. Pour over another layer of mousse and level using a palette knife, making sure the mousse reaches the cake collar. Return to the freezer until completely frozen and refrigerate the remaining mousse for use as garnish. At this stage, the cake may be frozen for up to 2 weeks.

(9) Remove the cake from the freezer 30 minutes before serving and release the baking ring. Place an alternating ring of plain and chocolate meringue buttons around the top of the cake. Pipe small buds of mousse on top of the cake using a pastry bag with a 1/4-inch open star tip and sprinkle with the remaining grated chocolate. Remove the cake collar and serve. May be stored for up to 3 days in the refrigerator.

Concorde

A staple in cafés all over France, my own version of this classic is easy to make in a home kitchen.

Serves 10

1 recipe Italian Meringue Mixture (Basics page 20)

1/2 cup confectioner's sugar

2 cups whipping cream

4 ounces bittersweet chocolate, cut in small pieces

2 tablespoons brandy

6 ounces white chocolate, cut in small pieces

Parchment paper

2 baking sheets, one of which fits into your freezer

Pastry bag with a 1/4-inch round tip

Electric mixer

Double boiler

10-inch baking ring

Cellophane cake collar

(1) Preheat the oven to 275°F. Draw two 10-inch circles on the underside of a piece of parchment paper and use it to line a baking sheet. These circles will guide you in Step 3. Line a baking sheet that fits into your freezer with parchment paper and set aside.

(2) Prepare the meringue mixture according to the recipe directions and transfer to a pastry bag with a 1/4-inch round tip.

(3) Working from the outside in, pipe two 10-inch filled discs of the mixture onto the baking sheet. Use the remaining mixture to pipe several 4-inch strips on the baking sheet. These strips will be used to decorate the cake, so make as many as you can.

(4) Sprinkle the confectioner's sugar passed through a strainer over the batter and bake for 2 hours. Transfer the meringue, with the parchment paper, to a wire rack and cool for 30 minutes.

(5) To make the bittersweet chocolate mousse, place 1 cup of the whipping cream in the bowl of an electric mixer and, using the whisk attachment, whip until almost stiff. Melt the bittersweet chocolate in the top of a double boiler. Using a rubber spatula, fold the melted chocolate and 1 tablespoon of the brandy into the whipped cream until smooth. Place in the refrigerator until ready to use.

(6) To make the white chocolate mousse, whip the remaining cup of whipping cream until almost stiff. Melt the white chocolate in the top of a double boiler. Using a rubber spatula, fold the melted chocolate and the remaining tablespoon of brandy into the whipped cream until smooth. Place in the refrigerator until ready to use.

(7) Line a 10-inch baking ring with a cellophane cake collar and place on the baking sheet that fits into your freezer.

(8) Gently press one of the meringue discs into the bottom of the baking ring. Pour a 1/2-inch layer of bittersweet chocolate mousse evenly over top and level with a rubber spatula. Place in the freezer for 20 minutes.

(9) Remove the cake from the freezer and place another meringue disc over top. Cover with a 1/2-inch layer of white chocolate mousse and level with a palette knife, making sure the mousse reaches the cake collar. Return to the freezer until completely frozen and refrigerate the remaining mousse for use as garnish. At this stage, the cake may be frozen for up to 2 weeks.

(10) Remove the cake from the freezer 30 minutes before serving and remove the baking ring and cake collar. Frost the sides and top of the cake with the remaining white chocolate mousse, and stick on the meringue fingers, with the side that touched the parchment paper facing outward, in a random asymmetrical style. Serve immediately or store for up to 3 days in the refrigerator.

Baba au Rhum

I can think of no better way to end this chapter than with the Baba au Rhum. Baba, which means "falling over" or "dizzy" in French, are small cakes made from a yeast dough.

Makes 12

2 tablespoons crumbled fresh or dry yeast

2 tablespoons sugar

1/2 cup milk

4 eggs

1 3/4 cups unbleached all-purpose flour

1/2 cup butter, room temperature

1/2 teaspoon salt

3 cups water

2 cups sugar

1/3 cup dark rum

1 cup whipping cream

1/4 cup confectioner's sugar

Dash of pure vanilla extract, optional

Large bowl

Baking sheet

Parchment paper

12 individual brioche molds

Saucepan

Medium bowl

Pastry bag with a 1/4-inch open star tip

(1) In a large bowl, combine the yeast, sugar, milk, and eggs. Whisk the mixture with a hand whisk until very smooth.

(2) Switch to a wooden spoon, and add the flour, butter, and salt. Continue mixing until the consistency has a texture between a batter and a dough.

(3) Cover with plastic wrap and set aside in a warm place, away from drafts, for 2 hours.

(4) Line a baking sheet with parchment paper and grease 12 individual brioche molds. Spoon the batter evenly into the molds, filling them 2/3 full. Place the molds on the lined baking sheet and set aside in a warm place for 1 hour.

(5) Preheat the oven to 375°F. Leave the brioche molds on the tray and bake for 20 minutes. Remove the cakes from the molds, and let cool on a wire rack for 20 minutes.

(6) In the meantime, combine the water and sugar in a saucepan and bring to the boil. Do not stir. Remove from heat, and stir in the rum.

(7) Put the cooled cakes in a pan with high sides, and pour the hot syrup over. Let cool at room temperature for 20 minutes, then chill in the refrigerator for 2 hours.

(8) In a medium bowl, whip the whipping cream, confectioner's sugar, and vanilla until stiff.

(9) Remove the cakes from the refrigerator, and use a sharp chef's knife to cut off the top of each one. Set the tops aside.

(10) Make a little well in each cake by removing a small amount from the center with a sharp knife.

(11) Put the whipped cream in a pastry bag with a 1/4-inch open star tip, and pipe a generous amount in the well of each cake. Close with the reserved tops and serve. May be stored up to 2 days in the refrigerator.

Note: For best results, I recommend using fresh yeast, rather than standard dry yeast, for this recipe. Fresh yeast is available in many supermarkets and specialty stores, and yields a more flavorful cake with a far better texture. Soak the finished cakes in a large amount of syrup, and be generous with the rum.

Génoise: Mousse & Crème Cakes

Mousse and crème cakes are my favorite of all patisserie. The names and descriptions of the cakes in this chapter may seem daunting, but once you get started you'll find that they are actually not so hard. You will need considerable preparation time, and some of the steps are quite advanced, but if you follow the steps carefully (no shortcuts!) you'll receive spectacular results — impressive cakes you'll be proud to serve to special guests and at every festive occasion.

Please feel free to improvise by changing a mousse or crème layer to suit your own personal taste. Just remember to use the same quantities as listed in the recipe, and read the recipe through before you begin. You might want to prepare some steps several days in advance, adding the final touches on the day of the event.

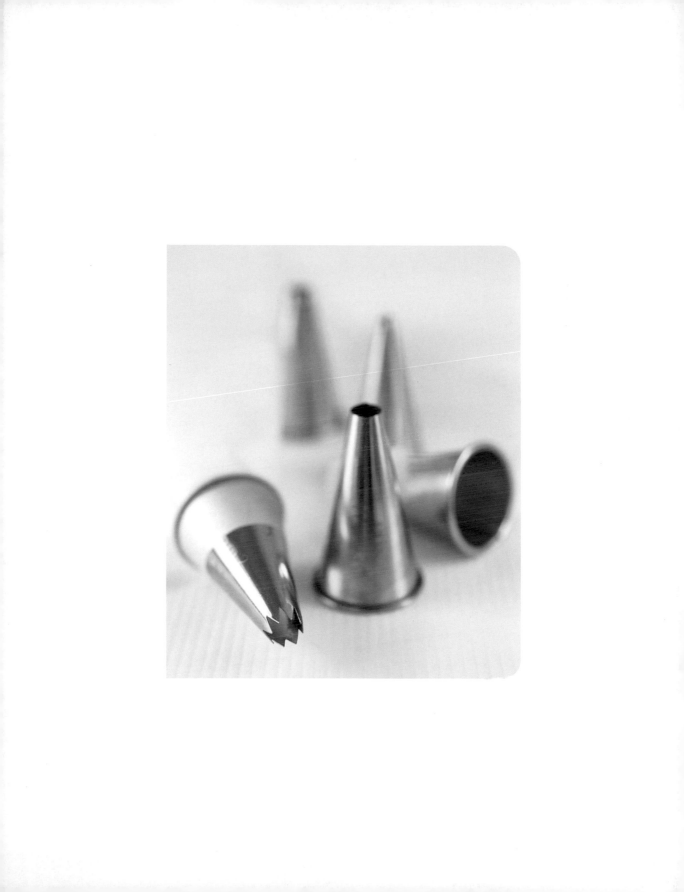

Fraisier

This cake is a real crowd pleaser—a winning combination of fresh strawberries, vanilla cream, and génoise. It is lovely to look at and delicious to eat. If you like, you can prepare the génoise a day in advance to cut down on preparation time.

Serves 10

1 recipe Basic Génoise Torte
(Basics page 17)

1/4 cup sugar

1/4 cup water

1 tablespoon schnapps or
fruit liqueur, any flavor

1 cup whipping cream

2 cups Crème Patissière
(Basics page 23)

30–35 medium strawberries,
washed

1/4 cup confectioner's sugar,
for garnish

2 baking sheets, one of
which fits into your freezer

Parchment paper

10-inch baking ring

Small saucepan

Electric mixer

Cellophane cake collar

Pastry bag with a 1/4-inch
round tip

(1) Preheat the oven to 375°F. Line 2 baking sheets with parchment paper. One will be used for baking, and the other must be able to fit into your freezer.

(2) Grease a 10-inch baking ring and place on the baking sheet that fits into your oven.

(3) Prepare the génoise according to the recipe directions and pour into the baking ring, filling it 2/3 full.

(4) Bake for 30 minutes, or until a toothpick inserted in the center comes out clean. Place the cake, with the baking ring, on a wire rack and cool for 30 minutes.

(5) To make the sugar syrup, combine the sugar and water in a small saucepan and bring to a boil over medium heat. Do not stir. Remove from heat and let stand at room temperature for 20 minutes. Stir in the schnapps.

(6) Place the whipping cream in the bowl of an electric mixer and, using the whisk attachment, whip till almost stiff. Use a small whisk to blend in the pastry cream till smooth.

(7) With a sharp knife, slice off the top of each strawberry at the point where it begins to widen. Place the strawberries cut-side down on a work surface.

(8) Remove the cake from the baking ring. Using a sharp serrated knife, slice the cake crosswise in the middle into 2 equal layers.

(9) Line the 10-inch baking ring with a cellophane cake collar and place on the baking sheet that fits into your freezer.

(10) Gently press one of the cake layers into the bottom of the baking ring and pour the sugar syrup evenly over top.

(continued on page 154)

(11) Transfer the cream mixture to a pastry bag with a 1/4-inch round tip and pipe evenly onto the cake in a spiral pattern, working from the center outward, and stopping about 1/4 inch from the edge of the cake.

(12) Lay the strawberries along the edge of the cake so that the cut sides are touching the cake collar. Work toward the center making additional rings of strawberries.

(13) Pipe more filling over and between the strawberries to cover them, and top with the second layer of cake, like a sandwich. Place a heavy plate on top of the cake to weigh it down, and place in the freezer for 30 to 45 minutes. At this stage, the cake may be frozen for up to 2 weeks.

(14) Just before serving, remove the baking ring and sprinkle the top with a generous amount of confectioner's sugar passed through a strainer. Remove the cake collar and serve. May be stored for up to 3 days in the refrigerator.

Tricolor Chocolate Torte

A staple in most European bakeries, this festive torte was one of my favorites as a child. The process seems complicated, and although it's time-consuming, it's actually quite easy to make—something for ten really special (and lucky) guests!

Serves 10

1 recipe Ladyfinger Mixture (Basics page 18), with 1 tablespoon cocoa

1/4 cup sugar

1/4 cup water

5 ounces bittersweet chocolate, cut in small pieces

3 3/4 cups whipping cream

(1) Preheat the oven to 375°F. Draw a 10-inch circle on the underside of a piece of parchment paper and use it to line a baking sheet. This circle will guide you in Step 3. Line a baking sheet that fits into your freezer with parchment paper and set aside.

(2) Prepare the ladyfinger mixture, with the cocoa, according to the recipe directions and transfer to a pastry bag with a 1/3-inch round tip.

(3) Working from the outside in, pipe a 10-inch filled disc of the mixture onto the baking sheet and bake for 20 minutes, or until golden brown. Transfer the cake, with the parchment paper, to a wire rack and cool for 30 minutes.

(continued on page 156)

3 3/4 cups whipping cream

5 ounces milk chocolate, cut in small pieces

6 ounces white chocolate, cut in small pieces

1 tablespoon cocoa, for garnish

Parchment paper

2 baking sheets, one of which fits into your freezer

Pastry bag with a 1/3-inch round tip

Small saucepan

10-inch baking ring

Cellophane cake collar

Double boiler

Electric mixer

(4) To make the sugar syrup, combine the sugar and water in a small saucepan and bring to a boil over medium heat. Do not stir. Remove from heat and let stand at room temperature for 20 minutes.

(5) Line a 10-inch baking ring with a cellophane cake collar and place on the baking sheet that fits into your freezer.

(6) Turn the cake over onto a work surface so that the parchment paper is facing up and carefully peel off the paper. (If the cake breaks, all is not lost—you can still stick the pieces together.)

(7) Gently press the cake into the bottom of the baking ring, with the side that touched the parchment paper facing up, and pour the sugar syrup evenly over top.

(8) To make the bittersweet chocolate mousse, melt the bittersweet chocolate in the top of a double boiler. Place 1 1/4 cups of the whipping cream in the bowl of an electric mixer and, using the whisk attachment, whip till almost stiff. Using a rubber spatula, fold the melted chocolate into the whipped cream till smooth.

(9) Pour the mousse evenly over the cake, level with a rubber spatula, and place in the freezer for 20 minutes.

(10) To make the milk chocolate mousse, melt the milk chocolate in the top of a double boiler. Whip 1 1/4 cups of the whipping cream till almost stiff. Using a rubber spatula, fold the melted chocolate into the whipped cream till smooth.

(11) Remove the cake from the freezer and pour the mousse over top, leveling it with a rubber spatula. Return to the freezer for 20 minutes.

(12) To make the white chocolate mousse, melt the white chocolate in the top of a double boiler. Whip the remaining 1 1/4 cups whipping cream till almost stiff. Using a rubber spatula, fold the melted chocolate into the whipped cream till smooth.

(13) Remove the cake from the freezer and pour the mousse over top, leveling it with a palette knife, and making sure the mousse reaches the cake collar. Return to the freezer till completely frozen. At this stage, the cake may be frozen for up to 2 weeks.

(14) Just before serving, remove the baking ring and sprinkle the top with cocoa passed through a strainer. Remove the cake collar and serve. May be stored for up to 3 days in the refrigerator.

Caramel Hazelnut Torte

Hazelnuts and caramel are always a winning combination, but the addition of chocolate makes this mixture simply divine. You can make these cakes a week or two in advance, and defrost and garnish just before serving.

Makes 5

1 recipe Ladyfinger Mixture
(Basics page 18)

2 tablespoons water

3/4 cup sugar

3/4 cup finely chopped
hazelnuts

2 cups whipping cream

9 ounces bittersweet
chocolate, cut in small
pieces

4 ounces bittersweet
chocolate, grated, for garnish

Parchment paper

2 baking sheets, one of
which fits into your freezer

Pastry bag with a 1/3-inch
round tip

Small saucepan

Five 3-inch baking rings

Cellophane cake collars

Electric mixer

(1) Preheat the oven to 375°F. Draw ten 3-inch circles on the underside of a piece of parchment paper and use it to line a baking sheet. These circles will guide you in Step 3. Line a baking sheet that fits into your freezer with parchment paper and set aside.

(2) Prepare the ladyfinger mixture according to the recipe directions and transfer to a pastry bag with a 1/3-inch round tip.

(3) Working from the outside in, pipe ten 3-inch filled discs of the mixture onto the baking sheet and bake for 20 minutes, or until golden brown. Transfer the cakes, with the parchment paper, to a wire rack and cool for 30 minutes.

(4) In the meantime, place 1/2 cup of the sugar in a small saucepan and cook till light brown. Add 1/2 cup of the hazelnuts, mix well, and cook on low heat for 10 minutes, or until the hazelnuts are light brown. Pour out onto a greased work surface and cool for 30 minutes, then chop into small pieces using a chef's knife.

(5) To make the ganache, combine the water and the remaining 1/4 cup sugar in a small saucepan and cook over medium heat until dark brown and caramelized. Do not stir. Remove from heat and, using a hand whisk, blend in 1 cup of the whipping cream and the 9 ounces of chocolate till smooth.

(6) Line five 3-inch baking rings with cellophane cake collars and place on the baking sheet that fits into your freezer.

(7) Carefully remove the cake discs from the parchment paper and gently press one disc into the bottom of each ring, with the side that touched the parchment paper facing up. Pour the ganache evenly over the top of each cake and place in the freezer for 20 minutes.

(8) To make the caramel hazelnut mousse, place the remaining cup of whipping cream in the bowl of an electric mixer and, using the whisk attachment, whip till almost stiff. Fold in the chopped hazelnut mixture using a rubber spatula.

(9) Remove the cakes from the freezer and place a cake disc on top of each cake. Pour the mousse on top and level with a palette knife, making sure the mousse touches the cake collars. Return to the freezer for at least 1 hour. At this stage, the cakes may be frozen for up to 2 weeks.

(10) Remove the cakes from the freezer 20 minutes before serving. Take off the baking rings and cake collars and wait 5 minutes for the sides of the cakes to thaw. With the palms of your hands, gently press the remaining 1/4 cup of hazelnuts around the sides of the cakes. Sprinkle the grated chocolate over top and serve. May be stored for up to 3 days in the refrigerator.

Jamaican Torte

This festive cake is an almost whimsical interplay of chocolate and coffee, two all-time favorite flavors. It's perfect for any occasion—even as a birthday cake.

Serves 10

1 recipe Ladyfinger Mixture (Basics page 18), with 1 tablespoon cocoa

3 cups whipping cream

3 tablespoons Coffee Essence (Basics page 29)

5 ounces bittersweet chocolate, cut in small pieces

4 ounces milk chocolate, cut in small pieces

1/4 cup sugar

1 tablespoon coffee liqueur

1/2 cup Royal Chocolate Frosting (Basics page 21)

(1) Preheat the oven to 375°F. Draw a 10-inch circle on the underside of a piece of parchment paper and use it to line a baking sheet. This circle will guide you in Step 3. Line a baking sheet that fits into your freezer with parchment paper and set aside.

(2) Prepare the ladyfinger mixture, with the cocoa, according to the recipe directions and transfer to a pastry bag with a 1/3-inch round tip.

(3) Working from the outside in, pipe a 10-inch filled disc of the mixture onto the baking sheet and bake for 20 minutes, or until golden brown. Transfer the cake, with the parchment paper, to a wire rack and cool for 30 minutes.

(4) To make the coffee ganache, place 1 cup of the whipping cream and 1 tablespoon of the coffee essence in a small saucepan and bring to a boil. Remove from heat and pour over the bittersweet chocolate. Blend with a hand whisk till smooth.

(5) Line a 10-inch baking ring with a cellophane cake collar and place on the baking sheet that fits into your freezer.

(6) Turn the cake over onto a work surface so that the parchment paper

Parchment paper

2 baking sheets, one of which fits into your freezer

Pastry bag with a 1/3-inch round tip

Small saucepan

10-inch baking ring

Cellophane cake collar

Double boiler

Electric mixer

is facing up, then carefully peel off the paper. (If the cake breaks, all is not lost—you can still stick the pieces together.)

(7) Gently press the cake into the bottom of the baking ring, with the side that touched the parchment paper facing up. Pour the ganache over top and place in the freezer for 30 minutes.

(8) To make the coffee chocolate mousse, melt the milk chocolate in the top of a double boiler. Place 1 cup of the whipping cream in the bowl of an electric mixer and, using the whisk attachment, whip till almost stiff. Using a rubber spatula, fold the melted chocolate and 1 tablespoon of the coffee essence into the whipped cream till smooth.

(9) Remove the cake from the freezer and pour the mousse over top. Level with a rubber spatula and return to the freezer for 20 minutes.

(10) To make the coffee mousse, whip the remaining cup of whipping cream with the sugar till almost stiff. Using a rubber spatula, fold in the remaining tablespoon of coffee essence and the coffee liqueur till smooth.

(11) Remove the cake from the freezer and pour the mousse over top. Level with a palette knife, making sure the mousse reaches the cake collar. Return to the freezer for at least 1 hour. At this stage, the cake may be frozen for up to 2 weeks.

(12) Remove the cake from the freezer 30 minutes before serving. Immediately remove the baking ring, and spread chocolate frosting on top of the frozen cake. Remove the cake collar, thaw for 30 minutes, and serve. May be stored for up to 3 days in the refrigerator.

Ambroisie

As its name suggests, this cake is fit for the gods—and one of the most popular cakes in Paris. The flavors are complex and the frosting is heavenly. To simplify matters, I often make this cake over the course of several days, preparing a different mousse layer each day and freezing it.

Serves 10

1 recipe Ladyfinger Mixture (Basics page 18), with 1 tablespoon cocoa

3 cups whipping cream

15 ounces bittersweet chocolate, cut in small pieces

1/4 cup sugar

1/4 cup water

1/2 cup Marzipan (Basics page 30)

1 recipe Royal Chocolate Frosting (Basics page 21)

Parchment paper

2 baking sheets, one of which fits into your freezer

Pastry bag with a 1/3-inch round tip

10-inch baking ring

Cellophane cake collar

Double boiler

Electric mixer

(1) Preheat the oven to 375°F. Draw an 11-inch circle on the underside of a piece of parchment paper and use it to line a baking sheet. This circle will guide you in Step 3. Line a baking sheet that fits into your freezer with parchment paper and set aside.

(2) Prepare the ladyfinger mixture, with the cocoa, according to the recipe directions and transfer to a pastry bag with a 1/3-inch round tip.

(3) Working from the outside in, pipe an 11-inch filled disc of the mixture onto the baking sheet and bake for 15 minutes, or until golden brown. Transfer the cake, with the parchment paper, to a wire rack and cool for 30 minutes.

(4) To make the ganache, bring 1 cup of the whipping cream to a boil and remove from heat. Using a hand whisk, blend in 5 ounces of the chocolate till smooth. Set aside.

(5) To make the sugar syrup, combine the sugar and water in a small saucepan and bring to a boil over medium heat. Do not stir. Set aside to cool to room temperature.

(6) Turn the cake over onto a work surface so that the parchment paper is facing up and carefully peel off the paper. (If the cake breaks, all is not lost—you can still stick the pieces together.)

(7) Place the cake on a work surface and use a 10-inch baking ring to cut it into a 10-inch disc. Reserve the trimmed pieces for use in Step 13.

(8) Line the 10-inch baking ring with a cellophane cake collar and place on the baking sheet that fits into your freezer. Gently press the cake into the bottom of the ring.

(continued on page 162)

160

(9)   Pour the sugar syrup evenly over the cake, and pour the ganache over top. Place in the freezer for 20 minutes.

(10)   To make the chocolate marzipan mousse, melt 5 ounces of the chocolate and the marzipan in the top of a double boiler. Place 1 cup of the whipping cream in the bowl of an electric mixer and, using the whisk attachment, whip till almost stiff. Using a rubber spatula, fold the melted chocolate mixture into the whipped cream till smooth.

(11)   Remove the cake from the freezer, pour the mousse over top, and level with a rubber spatula. Return to the freezer for 20 minutes.

(12)   To make the chocolate mousse, melt the remaining 5 ounces of chocolate in the top of a double boiler. Whip the remaining cup of whipping cream till almost stiff. Using a rubber spatula, fold the melted chocolate into the whipped cream till smooth.

(13)   Remove the cake from the freezer and place the cake pieces reserved in Step 7. Pour the mousse over top, leveling it with a palette knife and making sure it reaches the cake collar. Return to the freezer till completely frozen. At this stage, the cake may be frozen for up to 2 weeks.

(14)   Remove the cake from the freezer 30 minutes before serving. Immediately take off the baking ring and cake collar and pour a generous amount of chocolate frosting on top of the frozen cake. Using a palette knife, spread the icing over the top and sides of the cake. It is important to work quickly while spreading the icing, because it tends to harden on contact with the frozen cake. Let the cake thaw for 30 minutes and serve. May be stored for up to 3 days in the refrigerator.

Praline Torte

This is a relatively easy mousse cake to make, and while I've included only 2 tablespoons of Amaretto in the recipe, you might want to add more to suit your taste.

Serves 10

1 recipe Ladyfinger Mixture (Basics page 18)

2 cups whipping cream

1/2 cup Nutella or other nut spread

2 tablespoons Amaretto

9 ounces bittersweet chocolate, cut in small pieces

3/4 cup coarsely chopped toasted hazelnuts

Parchment paper

2 baking sheets, one of which fits into your freezer

Pastry bag with a 1/3-inch round tip

Electric mixer

Small saucepan

10-inch baking ring

Cellophane cake collar

(1) Preheat the oven to 375°F. Draw two 10-inch circles on the underside of a piece of parchment paper and use it to line a baking sheet. These circles will guide you in Step 3. Line a baking sheet that fits into your freezer with parchment paper and set aside.

(2) Prepare the ladyfinger mixture according to the recipe directions and transfer to a pastry bag with a 1/3-inch round tip.

(3) Working from the outside in, pipe two 10-inch filled discs of the mixture onto the baking sheet and bake for 15 minutes, or until golden brown. Transfer the cakes, with the parchment paper, to a wire rack and cool for 30 minutes.

(4) To make the Nutella Amaretto mousse, place 1 cup of the whipping cream in the bowl of an electric mixer and, using the whisk attachment, whip till almost stiff. Using a hand whisk, blend in the Nutella and Amaretto until smooth and place in the refrigerator for 30 minutes.

(5) To make the ganache, bring the remaining cup of whipping cream to a boil in a small saucepan. Remove from heat and, using a hand whisk, blend in the chocolate and 1/2 cup of the toasted hazelnuts until smooth.

(6) Line a 10-inch baking ring with a cellophane cake collar and place on the baking sheet that fits into your freezer.

(7) Turn the cakes over onto a work surface so that the parchment paper side is facing up and carefully peel off the paper. (If they break, all is not lost—you can still stick the pieces together.)

(8) Gently press one of the cakes into the bottom of the baking ring, with the side that touched the parchment paper facing up. Pour the ganache evenly over top and place in the freezer for 20 minutes.

(9) Remove the cake from the freezer and place the other cake over top. Pour the mousse over the cake and level with a palette knife. Return to the freezer till completely frozen. At this stage, the cake may be frozen for up to 2 weeks.

(10) Remove the cake from the freezer 30 minutes before serving and take off the baking ring. Sprinkle the remaining 1/4 cup of hazelnuts over top and let thaw. Remove the cake collar and serve. May be stored for up to 3 days in the refrigerator.

Chestnut Torte

This great torte celebrates the magical combination of white chocolate and candied chestnuts. Relatively easy to make, it can be prepared a few days in advance and frozen until ready to use. Remember to use the best quality candied chestnuts you can find.

Serves 10

1 recipe Ladyfinger Mixture (Basics page 18)

1 cup sugar

1/4 cup water

3 cups whipping cream

7 ounces white chocolate, cut in small pieces

3/4 cup candied chestnuts, minced

6-ounce block of white chocolate, for garnish

2 baking sheets, one of which fits into your freezer

Parchment paper

Pastry bag with a 1/3-inch round tip

Small saucepan

Bowl

Double boiler

Electric mixer

10-inch baking ring

Cellophane cake collar

(1) Preheat the oven to 375°F. Draw two 10-inch circles on the underside of a piece of parchment paper and use it to line a baking sheet. These circles will guide you in Step 3. Line a baking sheet that fits into your freezer with parchment paper and set aside.

(2) Prepare the ladyfinger mixture according to the recipe directions and transfer to a pastry bag with a 1/3-inch round tip.

(3) Working from the outside in, pipe two 10-inch filled discs of the mixture onto the baking sheet. Bake for 15 minutes, or until golden brown. Transfer the cakes, with the parchment paper, to a wire rack and cool for 30 minutes.

(4) To make the caramel syrup, combine the sugar with the water in a small saucepan and cook over medium heat till dark brown. Do not stir. Blend in 1 cup of the whipping cream and continue to cook over medium heat, stirring often, till thick. Transfer to a clean bowl and let stand at room temperature for 30 minutes.

(5) To make the white chocolate mousse, melt the white chocolate in the top of a double boiler. Place 1 cup of the whipping cream in the bowl of an electric mixer and, using the whisk attachment, whip till almost stiff. Using a rubber spatula, fold the melted chocolate into the whipped cream till smooth. Place in the refrigerator until ready to use.

(6) To make the chestnut mousse, whip the remaining cup of whipping cream till almost stiff. Using a rubber spatula, fold the candied chestnuts into the whipped cream until they are evenly distributed. Place in the refrigerator until ready to use.

(7) Line a 10-inch baking ring with a cellophane cake collar and place on the baking sheet that fits into your freezer.

(8) Turn the cakes over onto a work surface so that the parchment paper is facing up and carefully peel off the paper. (If they break, all is not lost–you can still stick the pieces together.)

(9) Carefully press one of the cakes into the bottom of the baking ring, with the side that touched the parchment paper facing up. Pour the caramel syrup evenly over top. Place in the freezer for 20 minutes.

(10) Remove the cake from the freezer and pour the white chocolate mousse over top. Level with a rubber spatula and return to the freezer for 20 minutes.

(11) Remove the cake from the freezer and place the other cake over top. Pour the chestnut mousse over the cake and level with a palette knife, making sure the mousse reaches the cake collar. Return to the freezer till completely frozen. At this stage, the cake may be frozen for up to 2 weeks.

(12) Remove the cake from the freezer 30 minutes before serving and remove the baking ring. Using a large vegetable peeler, make curls of white chocolate and place on top of the cake. Remove the cake collar and serve. May be stored for up to 3 days in the refrigerator.

Montmirail

This creation is a dreamy combination of dulce de leche, a traditional South American caramel spread found in gourmet supermarkets, and chestnuts. With its surprising chocolate center and white chocolate curls, it is a distinct dessert that will definitely impress your friends.

Serves 10

1 recipe Ladyfinger Mixture (Basics page 18)

1 1/2 cups dulce de leche

2 cups whipping cream

9 ounces bittersweet chocolate, cut in small pieces

1 cup candied chestnuts, coarsely chopped

2 tablespoons Amaretto

6-ounce block of white chocolate, for garnish

Parchment paper

3 baking sheets, one of which fits into your freezer

Pastry bag with a 1/3-inch round tip

Small saucepan

10-inch baking ring

Cellophane cake collar

Electric mixer

(1) Preheat the oven to 375°F. Draw two 10-inch circles on the underside of a piece of parchment paper and use it to line a baking sheet. These circles will guide you in Step 3. Line 2 more baking sheets with parchment paper. One will be used for baking and the other must be able to fit into your freezer.

(2) Prepare the ladyfinger mixture according to the recipe directions and transfer to a pastry bag with a 1/3-inch round tip.

(3) Working from the outside in, pipe two 10-inch filled discs of the mixture onto a baking sheet. Use a palette knife to spread the remaining mixture 1/8 inch thick to cover the other baking sheet. Bake both sheets for 15 minutes, or until golden brown. Transfer the cakes, with the parchment paper, to a wire rack and cool for 30 minutes.

(4) Turn the cakes over and carefully peel off the parchment paper. Place the rectangular cake on a work surface, with the side that touched the parchment paper facing up. Use a palette knife to spread 1 cup of the dulce de leche evenly over top. Working from the long side, roll up into a log, wrap in plastic wrap, and place in the freezer for 40 minutes.

(5) To make the ganache, place 1 cup of the whipping cream in a small saucepan and bring to a boil. Remove from heat and add the bittersweet chocolate. Blend with a hand whisk till smooth.

(6) Line a 10-inch baking ring with a cellophane cake collar and place on the baking sheet that fits into your freezer.

(7) Gently press one of the round cakes into the bottom of the baking ring, with the side that touched the parchment paper facing up.

(8) Remove the dulce de leche roll from the freezer and use a chef's knife to cut it into 1/8-inch-thick slices. Press a row of slices along the sides at the bottom of the baking ring. Make another row on top to cover the sides completely.

(9) Pour the ganache inside and level with a rubber spatula. Sprinkle 1/2 cup of the candied chestnuts on top, and place in the freezer for 20 minutes.

(10) To make the caramel Amaretto mousse, place the remaining cup of whipping cream in the bowl of an electric mixer and, using the whisk attachment, whip till almost stiff. Using a hand whisk, blend in the remaining 1/2 cup of Dulce de Leche and the Amaretto till smooth.

(11) Remove the cake from the freezer, and place the other cake on top. Pour the mousse over top, leveling it with a palette knife and making sure the mousse reaches the cake collar. Sprinkle the remaining 1/2 cup of candied chestnuts over top and return to the freezer till completely frozen. At this stage, the cake may be frozen for up to 2 weeks.

(12) Remove the cake from the freezer 30 minutes before serving and take off the baking ring. Using a large vegetable peeler, make curls of white chocolate and place on top of the cake. Remove the cake collar and serve. May be stored in the refrigerator for up to 2 days.

Index